Understanding the Nature of Autism
and Asperger's Disorder

Understanding the Nature of Autism and Asperger's Disorder

Forty Years of Clinical Practice and Pioneering Research

Edward R. Ritvo, MD

Foreword by Tony Attwood

Jessica Kingsley Publishers
London and Philadelphia

First published in 2006
by Jessica Kingsley Publishers
116 Pentonville Road
London N1 9JB, UK
and
400 Market Street, Suite 400
Philadelphia, PA 19106, USA

www.jkp.com

Library of Congress Cataloging in Publication Data
Ritvo, Edward, 1930-
Understanding the nature of autism and Asperger's disorder : forty years of clinical practice
and pioneering research / Edward R. Ritvo ; foreword by Tony Attwood.
    p. cm.
Includes index.
ISBN-13: 978-1-84310-814-6 (pbk. : alk. paper)
ISBN-10: 1-84310-814-3 (pbk. : alk. paper) 1. Autism. 2. Asperger's syndrome. I. Title.
RC553.A88R58 2005
616.85'8832—dc22
                        2005018076
British Library Cataloguing in Publication Data
A CIP catalogue record for this book is available from the British Library

ISBN-13: 978 1 84310 814 6
ISBN-10: 1 84310 814 3

Printed and bound in Great Britain by
Athenaeum Press, Gateshead, Tyne and Wear

I wish to dedicate this book to
Riva Ariella Ritvo, and to our three wonderful children,
Victoria, Skye, and Max.

Also, I respectfully dedicate this book to the memory of a
young man who died in an automobile accident in April
1999, and to his courageous parents who donated his organs
so others could live. I received his heart and treasure the gift
of life they provided for me. If this volume helps but one
person or family with autism or Asperger's disorder, or one
professional, or one student, then they too owe him and his
family a similar debt of gratitude.

Lastly, I wish to honor the memory of two men who shaped
my early life and guided my professional career, my father,
Max Ritvo MD, and my uncle, Joseph Weinreb MD.

"The quest to understanding others begins at the end of the road to self-acceptance."

Max Joseph Ritvo,
age 13 (2004)

Contents

List of Tables

List of Figures

Foreword

Over the last forty years, Edward Ritvo, MD has conducted many of the seminal research studies examining the medical aspects of autism. He observed and contributed to the dawn of our scientific knowledge on autism and Asperger's disorder that began in the late 1960s. Today, younger scientists and clinicians tend to focus on contemporary research and overlook some of the original studies. But new light can shine through old windows. As Edward Ritvo, MD describes the context for his original research and interprets the results, the reader becomes aware that the studies conducted twenty or thirty years ago are still contributing to our understanding of autism and our current theoretical models and treatments.

There are few people in the world that can use an historical perspective over many decades to perceive the changing conceptualization and treatment strategies of autism spectrum disorders. We need the wise council of Edward Ritvo, MD in such diverse areas as diagnosis, aetiology, treatment and especially prognosis. What autism is and what are its causes and treatments along with how children with autism can develop, are the central themes of this book.

Parents will be delighted to read the advice of an extremely experienced clinician, a realist and optimist, based on the personal experience of diagnosing, studying and treating thousands of children and adults whose expression of autism has ranged from severe to relatively mild. Of particular interest is the seminal description of adults with autism or Asperger's disorder who are parents. Clinicians first thought that someone with autism could never marry and have children. Over ten years ago, Edward Ritvo, MD documented and proved that someone with autism can experience an intimate and loving relationship with a partner and have children.

Clinicians will enjoy reading the descriptions of diagnostic procedures and the case studies, and appreciate the opportunity to re-evaluate Edward Ritvo, MD's original and current medical research studies. Those with autism or Asperger's disorder will also appreciate the respect the author has for their abilities and personalities. I hope that Edward Ritvo, MD writes subsequent editions of this book over the next decades.

Tony Attwood, author of the bestselling book
Asperger's Syndrome: A Guide for Parents and Professionals

Acknowledgments

First and foremost I wish to acknowledge my love and appreciation to my partner, Riva Ariella Ritvo. Not only has she been a key member of our research team over the years and assisted me in writing this book, she also guided me along a path to recovery when my heart failed six years ago. Her foresight was crucial to my having received a successful heart transplant operation, and her continued caring allowed me to recover my health and enjoy the years since. I also thank her for giving me our three wonderful children, Victoria, Skye, and Max. They are the "lights of my life."

Many thanks go to my colleagues from around the world who traveled with me down the research road. Some helped me forge ahead, some went alongside, and some firmed up paths I pioneered. Their names and contributions are cited in the chapters that describe our collaborative work.

And of course none of our research could have been done without the participation of my patients and their families. They literally gave us their days, their nights, their blood, their urine and sweat, and sometimes their tears. Their altruistic ability to participate in research projects that contributed to our understanding of autism in a general way, but was of no direct or immediate benefit to them, makes them worthy of sainthood in my eyes.

Also, a special thanks to my daughter Victoria for her contributions to the section on occupational therapy.

The following families generously offered financial support over the years: Dr. and Mrs. Tamkin, Mr. and Mrs. Benin, Gilbert, Kunin, Miano, Baker, and Zuckerman.

Finally, I wish to acknowledge my deep indebtedness to the heart of our UCLA team, those who stayed the course over the decades: Riva Ariella Ritvo, Professors Edward Ornitz, "B.J." Freeman, Art Yuweiler, Edward Geller and Don Guthrie, Mrs. Ann Mason Brothers, Mr. Eddie Carr, and our "bosses" Professors Henry Work, George Tarjan, and James Q. Simmons III.

Introduction

Why I'm writing this book

There are many reasons I'm putting pen to paper, or I should say, typing on my laptop. But far and away the most important is my wish to explain to everyone with autism and Asperger's disorder the basic nature of their disorder.

My own quest for understanding started in 1963, when I joined the faculty of UCLA Medical School as a young instructor. Armed with a newly earned Board Certificate in Child Psychiatry and enough enthusiasm to overcome the fact that I had no formal research training, I set out to slay the fire-breathing dragon we called at that time "atypical autistic ego development." Believe it or not, I have been jousting with this same mean dragon ever since. While it's far from dead, I've learned a lot about it over these past forty years, and I am eager to share that knowledge with each and everyone who battles this dragon every day of their life.

The second reason I'm writing this book is to give hope and understanding to the families and loved ones of all those who have autism and Asperger's disorder.

When I saw my first little child with what we now call severe autism I was still a medical student in Boston. It was 1954, and the diagnosis was tantamount to a death sentence; the equivalent of cancer. Seeing the fear and anxiety that overwhelmed parents when I had to tell them that their child had autism filled me with sadness and frustration. This is one of the most painful parts of our profession. Yet, let me hasten to add, with autism, there is good news too. As I shall explain later, I have learned over the years by watching hundreds of my patients grow from preschoolers to adults that such a pessimistic view was, and is, all wrong!

Our research, and other studies from around the world, have shown that without question, autism and Asperger's disorder are remittent. That means they naturally improve over time. Thus, there is always good reason for optimism and hope for the future for each and every person with either of these disorders.

I also want to give a warning. It is a sad fact that during the four decades that I have been wandering down the research trail I've seen many false and harmful theories and many "sure-fire cures" come and go. The most unfortunate part of such wrong information is that it builds false hope in patients and parents alike. And no one is more vulnerable to false hope than the victim of an illness or parents who have just learned that their child is ill.

With this sad history in mind, I promise I shall give you a clear view of the nature and life course of these disorders. You also deserve to know what to expect from the treatments we have available today. Such a realistic view can "vaccinate" you against being infected by false hopes and the painful letdown they eventually lead to.

I also want to assure you from the outset that all the information I'll give you about the nature of autism and Asperger's disorder is based on sound scientific medical research, and represents the consensus of physicians and researchers around the world today. If I refer to something speculative, or give you an opinion on something not yet confirmed, I will label it as such very, very clearly.

Third, I am also writing this book for my fellow professionals, the ones who provide diagnostic services, treatment, and education to all those with autism and Asperger's disorder. After all, it is the psychologists, teachers, social workers, caseworkers, nurses, occupational therapists, speech and language therapists, physical therapists, psychotherapists, and behavior therapists who provide the day-to-day hands-on care that makes the difference.

And, last but not least, I am writing this book for our students. In particular it is for those who, like me, are under the spell of the muse of research. In order to devote our careers to research we have to remain "wild-eyed" optimists, driven by hope. We are certain that one day we'll discover cures and ways to prevent diseases. And to get more personal, I am sure that one day soon we shall triumph over autism and Asperger's disorder just as we have triumphed over other childhood disorders, like polio.

What this book is not

Before we begin, I want to make it clear what this book is not. It is not a textbook in the usual sense of the word. Also, it is not a reference or resource book, and it is not a diagnostic or treatment manual. There are already many excellent books of these types that cover these subjects.

No, my point in writing this book is simply to provide you with an understanding of the basic nature of autism and Asperger's disorder. By "basic nature" I mean their history, how they affect lives, what is wrong in the brain, what are the causes, and what treatments we have and what we can expect from them. This is a tall order, but one that can be accomplished with a little time and a lot of thinking on both our parts.

An apology to my readers who have autism or Asperger's disorder

These next few words are for all my readers who have autism or Asperger's disorder. As you know, there are certain ways of thinking that come naturally and "make sense" to you, and some ways of thinking that are very difficult to follow and do not "just make sense." While this is generally true for everyone, for you such differences in thinking styles can be extreme and cause much trouble.

For instance, many of you have told me that you think only in concrete pictures, some notice colors, shapes, and sizes, and most can't remember anything about people. Others think in sequences of ideas that have to follow a special order to make sense, and others think in "time separated" blocks of thought. I shall be describing these types of thinking in detail later, and I hope that I can make it clear how and why this happens.

But the complaint I get most often is that figures of speech and analogies are particularly difficult to follow and to understand. By these I am referring to all types of ideas that compare one thing to another, or one part of a thing to one part of another thing. Although analogies and figures of speech may be confusing to you, they are generally very helpful for teaching and explaining, and I have used them throughout this book.

Here is a way one girl with Asperger's disorder told me she learned to deal with analogies and figures of speech. She said that if I said something like "I am just whistling in the dark," she immediately sees me in her mind with my lips pursed and tries to hear the sound of my whistling in her head. Now, after learning about her difficulty with this type of symbolic thinking, she would say to herself, "He doesn't really mean that – that's silly, he knows, and I know it's not really dark and he is not really whistling. I'll ask him what he means and try to remember it so next time I won't have to ask." She went on to say that to help herself she has learned to ignore her first response to what she hears, and then tries to remember to look for another meaning. She has memorized most of the figures of speech she hears so she rarely has to ask.

Another young man with Asperger's disorder told me that when he hears an analogy he tries to figure out "what part of the first part of the analogy is being compared to what part of the second part of the analogy." For example, while we were talking I compared his brain to a computer. He told me he forced himself not to think of everything he knew about computers, pictures of which first flooded his mind when he heard me say "computer." Rather, he consciously made himself think of one thing about his computer that was like one thing about his brain. The fact that the brain and the computer are made up of many independent parts that are tied together to give them a similar "structure" was the clue that allowed him to make sense of my analogy.

I hope these examples are helpful. In any event, please accept my apology in advance. Unfortunately, I can't get along without using figures of speech and analogies.

Chapter 1

Understanding How to Understand a Disease

The medical model of disease

Having grown up in Boston, I learned to ski and hiked in the White Mountains of New England before I started the first grade. This gave me a life-long appreciation for the bounties of nature. Thus, when I entered college and found out there was a mountaineering club I naturally rushed to join. I was young and fearless, or as my folks called me, "young and foolish." After working for half of each summer vacation to pay for the second half, I would head off with my pals for the Alps or British Columbia to climb unexplored snow-capped peaks.

The first thing we young mountaineers learned was that if we were going to return safely for the next semester we needed a really good map. It had to show us where we started, where we were going, what trails were known, where the unknown lay, and how to get back. Our lives were at stake, and mistakes could not be undone by saying "I'm sorry."

In the same way that a map is needed for exploring mountains, we need something to guide us on our "journey" toward understanding autism and Asperger's disorder. Fortunately there is just such a guide or "map" – the medical model of disease. On this map all the information about any disease can be placed into four separate but logically connected categories.

I first learned about the medical model of disease from my father when I was just beginning medical school. Fortunately for me he was a professor of radiology at Harvard Medical School, and I was just old enough to accept that he knew more than I did, about medicine at least. Here is the map he explained to me (Figure 1). Please take a moment to understand its parts and the way they are connected, as it will help you to keep track of what we shall explain about the nature of autism and Asperger's disorder.

Symptoms ⟶	Pathology ⟶	Causes ⟶	Treatment
The things that bother us, which lead to pain, fevers, etc., we call symptoms	Symptoms are expressions of abnormal physical changes we call pathology	Pathology is due to one or more causes	Two types: 1. "Rational treatment" stops the exact cause 2. "Supportive treatment" helps nature provide the cure

Figure 1 The medical model of a disease

Let's take common childhood disease and see how this model helps organize our thinking. Pretend that Mrs. XYZ calls our office worried about her five-year-old girl, Suzie.

First, we ask what are Suzie's *clinical symptoms?* Mrs. XYZ tells us Suzie woke up in the middle of the night with a sore throat, a cough, and a fever of 103.5. "Bring her right in," we say.

Second, we ask ourselves, "What *pathology* (abnormal physical changes in her body) could be causing these symptoms?" An exam reveals Susan has enlarged red tonsils with white patches, swollen lymph nodes in her neck, and thick mucus in her throat. These abnormal findings explain her symptoms, and narrow our search for the culprit.

Third, now we can move on to figure out the *cause*. A swab of her throat is sent off to the lab to make a culture. And to no one's surprise, out grows beta strep bacteria. Mystery solved, she has a classic case of "strep" throat!

Fourth and finally, only now that we have a diagnosis can we move on to consider *treatment*. Luckily for Little Suzie, the lab also tells us that her bugs are sensitive to good old penicillin. We give her this tried and true antibiotic, bed rest, lots of fluids, aspirin, and cough syrup. In 48 hours she is her five-year-old self again.

This is how we shall organize all our information about autism and Asperger's disorder in the chapters ahead. First the clinical picture, then the brain pathology, then the causes, and finally the treatments.

Here is a final word about treatment in general. In medicine we have only two types. First, there are those aimed at removing or fighting the cause of a disease. These we call "rational treatments." Second, we have "supportive treatments." These are aimed at helping Mother Nature do her work. In Suzie's case we used both types. Penicillin was the rational treatment. Aspirin, bed rest, fluids, and cough syrup were the supportive treatments.

It is important to keep the distinction between these two types of treatment in mind when considering autism and Asperger's disorder. As I shall explain in detail later, we have not yet discovered a rational treatment for them, and all the treatments we do have are of the "supportive" type.

What did the Romans think?

One of the most fortunate "accidents" of my medical education was having a professor named Chester Keefer. He was an institution in his own right, having been the first to introduce penicillin into clinical practice in the United States just after World War II. He also was the Dean of The Boston University School of Medicine during the 1950s. Dr. Keefer was a true "physician." By this I mean he understood the nature of the illnesses he treated, their course, and how they affected the lives of each patient differently. He made us become devout students of the history of medicine. He would not let us discuss a disease unless we knew what the Egyptians called it, what the Greeks and Romans thought it was caused by, and how it was treated during the Dark Ages. If it was a disease named after a person, we had to know who that person was and why they were so honored, or cursed, as to have their name attached to a disease.

Of course, we wise medical students thought old Dr. Keefer was just an old fossil, a history addict, and was wasting our time. But soon enough his wisdom proved its worth. Each time I saw a patient with an unfamiliar disease and dug out its historical roots, I gained a new respect for the patient as well as for the disease. Each patient represented a link in a chain of suffering people that stretched back to antiquity. Each patient had unique symptoms and unique expressions of their disease, but each also had common characteristics that were typical of their disease. From this perspective I learned to appreciate how one disease can have many forms, how it could disguise itself over time, and how it could even masquerade as another disease. And finally, I learned to appreciate the fact that every disease has severe to mild forms. To this day I insist that all my students have a historical picture of every disease they diagnose and treat.

Likewise, our journey to understand the nature of autism and Asperger's disorder begins with a look back. I want you to appreciate how our knowledge of these "mysterious" new disorders evolved. Where did the term "autism" come from, who was Asperger and why do we honor him by using his name today? These are some of the questions I'll now answer for you. So let's hasten over to the History Department and get started.

The Dark Ages of child psychiatry – before 1940

The Dark Ages of medicine – as far as child psychiatry goes – lasted up to the 1940s, a scant 60 years ago. Before then most children with severe developmental disabilities were lumped together as "mentally retarded" or "mentally defective." All too often they wound up in warehouses called "state hospitals," "developmental centers," or "asylums." If they had seizures or obvious causes for their brain damage such as infections, physical injuries, or birth defects they would be placed for life in hospitals for "epileptics." Most of these institutions provided precious little treatment, no education, and often subhuman living conditions. They were usually located far from the homes of the children, and visits by parents were discouraged. The label "snake pit" was not coined by accident. In my own early clinical experience I had the misfortune to visit several such institutions and remember to this day the feelings of nausea and disgust they engendered.

Professor Leo Kanner (1894–1981)

A glance at the history of science shows that some of the most remarkable discoveries of all time have been made by men with no special equipment other than a keen sense of observation who were driven by unquenchable curiosity. Copernicus, Darwin, and Newton all used just their eyes but rather than simply observing, or looking at, the world, were armed with curiosity, enormous powers of observation, and a desire to seek the truth. Therein lies the difference between just "looking" and "seeking". And so the story of autism and Asperger's disorder also starts with two men who were also just armed with curiosity, enormous powers of observation, and a desire to seek the truth.

Our story begins in Baltimore during the early 1940s. A pediatrician turned psychiatrist (there was no medical specialty of child psychiatry in those days) began taking a fresh look at a group of "mentally defective" children brought by their distraught parents. His name was Leo Kanner, and we all owe him a great debt of gratitude.

Dr. Kanner listened to the parents and observed their children with an open mind, bypassing the old notions of mental deficiency and irreversible chronic brain damage. Rather, he paid attention to certain common features of these children's development and the way they dealt with their world. He soon realized that they were not just "retarded." Rather they showed areas of normal intellectual development as well as areas of serious retardation. He also saw that they shared similar strange behaviors that they did over and over again, had similar peculiar interests, and had similar strange language development. But most interesting to him was the fact that they failed to develop normal ways of relating emotionally to their parents and to him. They seemed to remain emotionally isolated and unattached, indeed he noted some were more attached to toys and other objects than to their parents.

Now I am pretty sure Dr. Keefer had not taught Dr. Kanner. But, like all great physicians, they shared a love for the history of medicine and the wisdom it conveyed. This is why I am sure that Dr. Kanner was very familiar with the writings of a famous Swiss psychiatrist, Eugen Bleuler. This is because he borrowed Bleuler's term "autistic" to describe the fact that his young patients could not relate emotionally to others.

Dr. Bleuler had been working with adult patients who thought everything in the world related to themselves. Borrowing from the Latin root *auto* meaning self, Bleuler coined the term "autistic" as an adjective to describe this type of self-centered thinking. Borrowing from Bleuler, Kanner coined the phrase "autistic disturbances of affective [emotional] contact" to describe the condition of his patients who did not relate emotionally to others.

We have a tendency in our language to change adjectives into nouns. Thus, soon after Dr. Kanner's first paper appeared with the adjective "autistic" in the title, it quickly morphed into "autism": a thing. Now children had autism or were called autistic.

But where were all the adults and kids with autism before the 1940s? Those with severe autism were usually called idiots, imbeciles, elective mutes, or severely retarded. Those with mild autism were usually called mildly retarded, borderline retarded, psychotic, psychopaths, seriously emotionally disturbed, or schizophrenic.

In the case where these children had areas of normal intellectual functioning (islands of normal function, such as a prodigious memory for lists or musical talents) they were called *idiots savants*. This label became quite fashionable because it conjures up the fantasy of a genius locked inside a handicapped child. Too bad that is just a myth. What happens with these individuals is that they have a cognitive (thinking) skill that is relatively normal, and it gets used a lot. By way of explanation it is like a person with polio who uses a wheelchair. His normal unaffected arm muscles get very strong, but they do not get to be "superman" strong, just very strong regular ones. There is no such thing as "genius muscles."

Here is a well-known example of a severely autistic boy with a "savant skill" that illustrates this point. He was born in England and was noted by age four to be able to draw remarkably well for his young age. His drawings were actually exact copies, and he could copy almost anything, even perspective drawings. He was hailed as a budding artistic genius, became quite famous, and even sold a lot of pictures. Unfortunately, as he grew older his drawing proved to be quite repetitive and less and less accurate copies of what he observed.

Those with mild or "high-functioning" autism were also often misdiagnosed. They were simply written off as odd ducks, social misfits, loners, hermits, learning disabled, seriously emotionally disturbed, or worse, by their families and acquaintances. We doctors diagnosed them as borderline character disorders, schizophrenic, schizoaffective, sociopathic, or psychopaths.

I feel very sad when I think of all those whom we misdiagnosed years ago. While we were ignorant of the true nature of autism it does not do away with or excuse the harm we did. I have met literally hundreds of such unfortunate people over the past decades. Many were needlessly subjected to treatments that not only did not help, but also made their lives worse. To them, on behalf of myself and my professional colleagues, I offer a belated apology. I hope that, as we educate a new generation of professionals to properly identify these disorders, we will avoid similar mistakes in the future.

And there you have a brief history of how the term autism was born and grew up to become the household word it is today. Now let's turn our attention to the term "Asperger's disorder."

Professor Hans Asperger (1906–1980)

Call it a quirk of fate, but at the same time as Dr. Kanner was working in Baltimore, a young Austrian pediatrician, Dr. Hans Asperger, was studying a group of young adults who had very unusual problems that did not fit the usual diagnostic categories. Namely, they were what we now call "socially blind." They had difficulty reading social cues, related to others in an unusual manner, did not show normal empathy, had peculiar interests, and were said to be "clumsy" when young. Unlike Kanner's first cases, they all were said to have begun talking on time and all had normal intelligence.

Now obviously Dr. Asperger had not studied with Dr. Keefer. But he, like Kanner, was a good student of the history of medicine. He borrowed the same adjective from Bleuler as Kanner had. He coined the term "autistic psychopathy," to describe his patients' inability to relate emotionally to others. Unfortunately, he published his findings in 1944, in a German-language medical journal that went out of press during World War II. As fate would have it his work remained unappreciated until it was translated into English and republished in 1981 by Dr. Lorna Wing, a British child psychiatrist.

When we first learned of Dr. Asperger's work we wondered if he was simply describing mild cases of autism. We soon made the now obvious connection between what these two pioneers had observed. However, there were other child psychiatrists who suggested that Dr. Asperger had found a separate disease. The consensus among specialists around the world today is that Dr. Asperger had simply identified very mild cases of what Kanner had described.

When I helped revise and update the medical and psychiatric diagnostic manuals in the 1990s (the *10th International Classification of Diseases* (ICD-10) and the *Diagnostic and Statistical Manual* (DSM-IV)), we decided to honor Dr. Asperger. To do this, we added Asperger's disorder to the list of pervasive developmental disorders as a formal diagnostic category for those with very mild autism. In chapters 8 and 9 I shall spell out the diagnostic criteria and describe the unique problems of those who are diagnosed with autism and Asperger's disorder.

It is interesting to note that after World War II Dr. Asperger lived a long and professionally productive life practicing pediatrics in Vienna. Unfortunately, he never followed up on his earlier interest in mild autism and published no other papers on the subject.

Chapter 2

The Clinical Symptoms: From Severe Autism to Asperger's Disorder

Some general points

As alluded to at the end of the last chapter, when it was realized that autism ranged in severity from the most severe and earliest-appearing form that Kanner described to the milder later-appearing form that Asperger described, the terms "pervasive developmental disorder" and "autism spectrum disorder" were coined. This diagnostic category lumps all the forms together. It pays respect to the fact that they are all part of the same disease, regardless of their degree of severity.

Here are some very important facts about autism and Asperger's disorder.

1. They are both "developmental syndromes." This means that they are identified by how they affect a person's development. By definition, a syndrome can have many causes. For example, high blood pressure is a syndrome, and there are, as you can guess, many causes for high blood pressure. Pneumonia, the flu, and even diabetes are other common syndromes, each with many causes.

2. The developmental problems and the symptoms caused by autism and Asperger's disorder are due to abnormal development of certain parts of the brain. While I shall explain how we discovered this in chapter 4, I want to stress now that there is no single symptom, no single developmental problem, and no single

abnormal behavior that tells us a person has autism or Asperger's disorder. I wish it were that easy, but despite decades of research looking for such a "smoking gun" none has yet been found.

3.   We have found autism and Asperger's disorders in every corner of the world where we have looked. And they affect all races, and have no special respect or preference for social class, religion, education, or income level.

4.   Our best guess is that they occur in about 30 to 40 of every 10,000 people. Because we now have trained a generation of professionals who know how to recognize them, and because we are now counting even very mild cases, we know of more cases than we did years ago. This raises the question: Is there an epidemic of new cases occurring (is the incidence rising), or does it just look like there is an epidemic because we are finding previously overlooked cases (no change in prevalence)? This question is widely debated by researchers and parents today. My best guess, and I want to make sure you know this is just a guess, is that because we are better at finding and accurately diagnosing these disorders, it just looks like an epidemic. If my guess is correct then the rise in newly diagnosed cases will level out in the next few years as we finish picking up the previously overlooked ones, and more completely identify the new ones. The truth of the matter is that at this time no one knows the answer for sure. However, there are several large studies underway which, so far, support my "guess" that there is no true epidemic.

5.   They occur four to five times more often in males than females. I am sad to say that the reason for this is unknown, and that is in spite of decades of research. My best guess is based on my clinical experience that girls with autism are usually much more seriously affected. This could mean that more girl fetuses destined to become autistic do not make it through pregnancy, but rather are spontaneously aborted. If this were the case it would result in more males being born who eventually become autistic. This is just a guess, and, as I said before, whenever I make a guess, as opposed to telling you what most professionals agree upon, I shall make it very clear that it is a guess. The truth of the matter is we just don't really know why there are many more males. But there certainly are, no matter where in the world we look.

Early and late onset of symptoms

When Dr. Edward Ornitz and I began our research at UCLA in the early 1960s we were quite young and knew next to nothing about what was wrong with our young patients. We acknowledged our ignorance, and being a bit rebellious put aside what we had been taught about bad parenting and psychological trauma causing autism. We decided to begin afresh by just listening to parents describe their autistic children, and by just observing their kids for long periods of time to see what we could "seek".

It turned out that one of the most important questions we asked each family was: "When did you first feel in your heart there was something wrong with your child?" It soon became clear that their answers fell into two clear-cut groups.

First there were those who saw differences right from the start. We heard time and again the same phrase: "He never gazed at me when he nursed, he was in his own world right from day one." And these were comments from parents who had already had a normal child, so they knew what to expect. Just as often we heard: "He was normal in every way till he got to be about 16 to 20 months old. Then he stopped looking at us, stopped learning to talk, and retreated into a world of his own."

The kids who showed symptoms right from birth we said had *early-onset autism*. And those who seemed to have had a normal course of development and then showed symptoms around 16 to 20 months of age we said had *late-onset autism*. Interestingly, at that time we though that the early-onset kids had a worse outcome than those with a late onset. That proved not to be the case. We now know that the time of onset does not predict the eventual life course of a child.

Delays, plateaus, and spurts of brain development

A second crucial thing we learned by just listening to the parents was that their autistic children learned skills in an unusual manner. Instead of learning to walk, to talk, and relate to others in a smooth coordinated manner like their non-autistic siblings, their development was of the "stop-and-start" variety. In other words, instead of developing skills at the normal predictable time, with a smooth developmental curve looking like an airplane taking off, their growth curve looked like a drunken sailor staggering up a flight of stairs.

Time and time again we heard how their kids showed no progress for a while (gloom and sadness), then new skills "suddenly" appeared (hope and joy), then there would be no change for a while (more gloom and sadness), and then another spurt would gladden their hearts.

Along with these spurts and plateaus of development we also heard that the expected coordination of developing skills in different areas was missing. For example, in the normally developing child, milestones of motor development (sitting, crawling, walking, running), talking (babbling, simple words, repeating, spontaneous speech), and relating to people and objects go along together in a harmonious manner. This was not the picture the parents of our autistic kids painted. Rather, they portrayed kids who progressed OK in one area (sitting, standing, walking, and running), but plateaued in another (started to talk but did not make it past labeling objects for a year), while the third area, relating to people and objects, showed jerky but steady progress. It was if the conductor of the symphony of brain development couldn't keep the different sections of the orchestra playing together to the beat of the baton.

It soon became apparent that this stop-and-start development (with plateaus and spurts) and the dissociation of developmental pathways were the major hallmarks of autism and Asperger's disorder. This unusual type of development is not seen in any other disease I know. For example, if a child has only "mental retardation," the three developmental pathways (motor, language, and social) go hand in hand at a slow and coordinated rate. Similarly, when a child's brain is damaged in a car accident, previously normal functions may be lost depending on the part of the brain that is injured, and recovery depends on the initial severity of the trauma.

What we soon learned from our listening to parents is simply this: when you see or hear of a child who has irregular development with spurts and plateaus and separation of developmental pathways, you must think of autism or Asperger's disorder.

We drew some charts (Figure 2) to help you visualize the normal rate and coordination of the three developmental pathways. Contrast this to the charts of autistic and Asperger's children who show separations of the pathways and the stop-and-start nature of brain development that is typical of autism and Asperger's disorders.

Symptoms due to developmental delays

Sensory-motor delay

While listening to parents we also arranged to watch their kids through one-way mirrors. We recorded their behaviors for hours each day, seven days a week, in the light, in the dark with snooper scopes, while they were alone, while they were with their parents, with nurses, and with us.

We soon saw that they shared many repetitive behaviors. They did these for about the same amount of time per week if you observed them for several weeks. For example, those that flapped their hands did it for about the same number of hours each week, week after week. Those that were hooked on rubbing things with their fingers, or spinning things, or lunging back and forth, or flapping their fingers in front of their eyes had the same consistent weekly patterns.

This gave us a clue that their repetitive behaviors were internally driven, not under voluntary control, and could be modified (decreased) only to a point. They were like breathing. If I offered you a million dollars to hold your breath for an hour, you could not do it as the need to breath is internally driven.

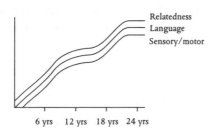

Normal development

Note smooth coordination of developmental pathways

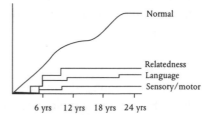

Severe autism

Note plateaus, a few spurts, and a separation of developmental pathways

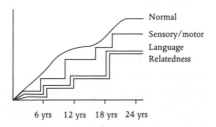

Mild/high-functioning autism

Note plateaus, spurts of development and separation of pathways

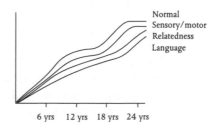

Asperger's disorder

Note Language and Relatedness lag, Sensory/motor near normal

Figure 2 *Comparison of developmental pathways in normal development, autism, and Asperger's disorder*

While watching the children so closely we were also struck by how they could change from being very sensitive to certain sensations to suddenly not responding at all. It was if their brain "tuned in" and then "faded out," like an old AM radio that couldn't stay exactly on a station.

This tuning in and out, responding and then not responding to the same sound for example, was so common that we concluded it was another hallmark of severe autism. Dr. Ornitz coined the term "perceptual inconstancy" to describe it in medical terms.

Here are some typical examples of what we now call "sensory-motor symptoms" as they affect each of the major senses. As you read about these symptoms try to imagine you have autism and you are tuning in and tuning out various sensations. What would it be like if the light went from so dim that you could hardly read this page to suddenly so bright it burned your eyes and you had to close them? Or imagine that I am whispering so softly you can barely hear what I am saying, then all of a sudden I am shouting loud enough to hurt your ears. That is what "perceptual inconstancy" means, and it is what autistic kids tell us in words and actions their sensory world is like.

Hearing

Many of our youngest autistic patients have had hearing tests before we see them. Here's how a typical initial interview with such a family goes:

"Why did you have Little Juan's hearing tested?" we ask.

"Grandma thought he was deaf because he didn't respond sometimes when she called his name. She even dropped a chair behind him one day and he didn't look around." said mother.

"Did you think he was deaf?" we ask.

"Oh no, because when Dad drives home and his tires creak softly on the pebbles in the driveway he always toddles to the door. If a plane flies by he looks out the window before we can even hear it. So I knew he wasn't deaf, but I had him tested anyway, you know – it just doesn't pay to argue with grandma, you know what I mean?"

Another hearing problem we hear about (pardon the pun) is supersensitivity to high-pitched noises. Vacuum cleaners, coffee grinders, and power tools can set off screaming tantrums. Seeing a kid wearing earmuffs on a hot bus in Los Angeles in the summer is a sure sign of autism.

Vision

The same child who bumps into chairs and tables as if not seeing them will later trace intricate designs in the sand. Staring off into space, flapping their fingers, sticks, or pencils before their eyes, flicking the wheels of little cars or toy trains and staring at them as they spin, looking out of the corner of their eyes, and peering up close to objects are all typical examples of visual "sensory motor play." When we hear that Junior knows exactly when *Wheel of Fortune* or *Jeopardy* come on the TV and insists on watching, well, the odds are he has autism. (The common denominator? It's the spinning wheel and the flashing lights.)

Vestibular sensations

Spinning around and staring at things that spin without getting dizzy are typical repetitive behaviors for autistics. When we hear that a child's favorite toy is a top, or that he spends hours spinning and staring at the wheels of a toy car, our index of suspicion of autism goes way up. Running toy trains back and forth on a piece of track, staring at ceiling fans and record players, and repetitive play with strobe lights are all typical repetitive behaviors of autistics. We know one patient with Asperger's disorder who worked as an electronic technician. She set up a strobe light in her lab and stared at it for a few minutes each hour every workday. She had another one at home for the weekends. She said it calmed her and helped her focus her thoughts. Jumping on trampolines is a behavior that also provides vestibular sensations and is a favorite with many children and adults.

Temperature regulation

The same child who insisted on wearing a coat indoors will later go outside and tear off their clothes while playing in the snow, and not get a single goose bump. We know autistic children who have picked up something hot and burned their hands without so much as a whimper.

Pain

Hard falls, deep cuts, and major skin scrapes can happen without the slightest evidence of pain. We have seen kids pinch their tiny fingers, raise a big black and blue bump, and then go on as if nothing happened. This lack of pain response can interfere with our diagnosing other illnesses. For example, there was a little autistic girl with appendicitis we learned about. She did not signal she was in pain and suffered for days before anyone figured out why she was not eating or drinking, and was having tantrums. Her pain threshold was very, very high.

I believe the brain systems in autism filter out the pain at certain times and thus the child does not respond appropriately, while at other times the brain amplifies the pain and makes it worse. It is the same with sound and other sensations; they are all subject to similar distortions. This brain process is called "perceptual inconstancy."

Smell

Many autistic children appear completely oblivious to bad odors at times, and then a day or two later overreact to the slightest odor. This was very embarrassing for a family we know when their four-year-old became insistent on pushing his nose into the lap of strangers and sniffing loudly. Temporary sensitivity to bathroom odors, cooking odors, and mother's perfumes are very common.

Position sense

Some autistic children can maintain set postures for a long time without moving. This is due to underresponsiveness to position sense (proprioception). In contrast, we can see writhing movements when they cannot maintain calm steady positions. Body rocking provides position sensations and can last for endless hours.

Taste

"He will only eat Big Macs," "He will only eat cheese pizza," "He will only eat pizza from one special Dominos," "She will only eat soft noodles," "He will only—." Such fussy food fads are so common they go without saying. These taste fads can change hourly, daily, or last for weeks.

Textures

Rubbing rough surfaces until their skin is red and bruised can give way to crying and fussing at the slightest touch. Stroking mother's hair, crinkling papers, and running water over their hands for hours on end are all done to achieve soft touch and texture sensations. Occupational therapists are frequently consulted to desensitize kids who are oversensitive to certain textures.

Another example of texture sensitivity is when a child will only eat soft, mushy foods. It is very common for young autistic children to go through a phase where all their food has to be blended in a food processor because they spit out anything with lumps in it. We tested this on several kids in our hospital program to see if it was the texture or the taste that led to the spitting out. It proved to be the lumps, the texture, and not the taste that determined what was spit out. I will spare you the details of the experiment, but will tell you that I had a very high laundry bill for dirty shirts while this experiment lasted.

All the symptoms we describe in this section are due to slow and irregular development of the part of the brain that modulates or regulates sensitivity and responses to sensations. None of these reactions is absolutely typical of autism, and they all can be seen in normally developing kids, albeit only for a short time. For example, all kids like to spin around, flap their hands, feel water and sand run through their fingers, jump up and down repeatedly, and jump at loud noises. In fact, we parents spend billions on toys and trips to Disneyland and Magic Mountain just to give our kids these sensations. (It sounds silly when I say it that way, but that is what we are paying for.) My point is, no one sensory motor behavior, or even several of them seen together, is unique to autism and Asperger's disorder.

What is unique, what we consider a hallmark of the disorder, is the going from over- to underreacting to sensations long after it should be outgrown. In other words, there is a developmental delay, a plateau, or a fixation of brain development at that immature level. Fortunately, the vast majority of autistics have spurts of brain development and leave these symptoms behind. Unfortunately, in rare cases, they can persist in to adulthood.

Delayed language development

In order to explain the delays in language that occur in autism and Asperger's disorder, I first have to give you a road map of normal development for comparison.

Normal language development

Since our model of normal language development begins during the first months of life we have to start off by agreeing that no one knows what newborns are thinking, or even if they are able to think in the usual sense of the word. But we can figure out what might be going on in their minds by closely observing their actions. Thus, the course of development of language I am about to map out is based on "infant watching." And when I speak for an infant, forgive me for taking a lot of "literary license." Here are the normal steps.

Step one: The Echo Phase. Baby is lying in his crib, just finished nursing, and starts to coo and babble. Random sounds gush forth: "Gooo Gooo, Baaa, Baaaa, Taaaa, Taaaaa, Maaaa, Maaaa."

"Did you hear that?" his excited mother exclaims, "He said Ma, Ma. He called me Ma, Ma! He said my name, Daddy, listen he said 'Ma Ma' I know his 'Ma Ma' was meant just for me." So gushes the typically objective mother. (Or father – I know I certainly did just this.)

Did you notice that mother has repeated Ma Ma several times? Soon she has repeated (echoed) baby's sounds of "Ma Ma" a dozen or more times while smiling, hugging, and picking up her little sweetheart for a cuddle. In this phase of language (brain) development the parents' echoing the baby is crucial.

Step two: The Echo/Labeling/Concrete Phase. Little Einstein, being nobody's fool, remembers those special sounds that got him his hugs and kisses, and echoes them to get more hugs and kisses. These reinforced and echoed "noises" we parents call his first "words." Of course, English babies echo English sounds, French babies French sounds, and so forth around the world. This is how we learn and pass on our "mother tongues."

For this stage to work we have to give baby power over us. Let me explain how we empower him. All he has to do is remember what sounds got him his hugs and kisses, say them back, and presto chango, we parents explode with joy, and he gets more hugs and kisses.

As baby is getting better and better at echoing his rote memory is also developing. Now he can remember specific sounds and tie them to specific people. "Ma Ma" is reserved for that nice big thing that hugs me and feeds me. "Da Da" is that big thing that picks me up, tosses me in the air, and scares me to death. In this way he learns to label his parents and all the objects he can see and touch.

By now we know a lot about what is going on in his brain just by watching and listening. He can hear, he can remember sound patterns, and he can control his vocal cords to reproduce specific sounds. And, this is crucial – he can remember and tie these sounds to objects and actions. That's what makes these sounds become words to us, his listeners.

To put this in terms of a computer model, we can observe that baby's big computer between his ears has input, memory, and output systems working. To repeat this in hopes of making it clearer, this is the stage when just echoing, labeling, and rote memory form the basis of language. Baby can repeat many things and tie them to what they represent in the world.

Words have only concrete meanings as they are attached to things he can see and touch.

Step three: The Symbolic Thinking Phase. In this phase we witness the dawn of a miracle that is unique to humans. Our toddler, now around two to two and a half years old, starts to understand abstract ideas. He can group objects by common features, can give meaning to abstract ideas and feelings, and can understand such subtle things as gestures.

In more technical terms he is attaching "symbolic meaning" to words and gestures. The best way to describe symbolic meaning is to think of two pieces of paper. One is blank; the other is printed by the government and says it is worth one hundred dollars. The plain piece has no symbolic value. The other can be traded in for lots of food, clothes, and whatever else costs up to one hundred dollars. It has a "symbolic value"; it represents or stands for things that are worth one hundred dollars.

Once children develop the capacity to assign symbolic value to words, they can use them to stand for something that is not touchable, seeable, smellable, or tasteable. The development of symbolic language is inherent, is automatic, is genetically programmed, and is essential if we are to communicate as human beings. It forms the basis for, and is the essence of, human thought.

Symbolic meaning allows us to take a certain feature of a thing and put it in a common class of things that share this feature. For example, *cars* and *airplanes* are symbolic words. Using them lets us group things that we get in and drive as "cars," and things that take us up in the air as "airplanes," even though not all cars and not all airplanes look alike. We also instinctually learn to attach symbolic meaning to abstract ideas and concepts that have no concrete counterpart at all. Guilt, shame, anger, joy, happiness, and empathy are totally symbolic concepts, no one has ever seen, smelled, or touched them.

As this stage progresses the child expands his ability to attach symbolic meaning to more and more sophisticated ideas. Symbolic meaning is given to specific people who bring comfort, and objects that represent these people. This is how "Mr. Teddy Bear" and "Special Pinky Blanket" get their magic. They symbolically represent mommy and bring back comforting memories of her to mind when we lock poor baby far away in the dungeon called his room at bedtime.

From this point on the brain develops rapidly, and soon the symbolic processing is so advanced that language in the usual sense of the word is present. This is when we begin to brainwash our kids in order to turn them in to little citizens. "NO" gets to be a big word. "No, don't put your finger in the light socket," "No, don't put your finger into your sister's eye," "No, don't say that," "No, you don't hate your oatmeal," "No, you can't poo poo and pee pee there." And, "You should be ashamed of yourself, don't you want other people to like you, what do you think grandmother would say about you if you did that?" and so on and so on. Such rules only work when and if junior has developed a symbolic sense (a mental image) of himself and how others think of him. Technically, we say he has developed the idea that other people have minds, have ideas of what he is like. This is called developing a "theory of mind." Much has been written about this idea and how it fails to develop normally in autism and Asperger's disorder.

To explain this stage in other words, it is when sophisticated and highly symbolic concepts spontaneously emerge. The child can learn what shame, guilt, remorse, loneliness, and needing to please to get love and attention are all about. The concept that others have thoughts, feelings, and a mind of their own, and that they think like him also emerges spontaneously.

When all is developing on schedule different types of thinking come online naturally. You can think in pictures, hear music in your mind, fit words to music, integrate colors, shapes, and textures of objects into meaningful memories, all in ways that are spontaneous and natural. Unfortunately, those with autism and Asperger's disorder cannot always do this, as we shall see.

Finally, at the end of this stage of language development the brain acts as a smoothly functioning symphony orchestra. The memory section holds the score, the emotion section turns the volume up and down, and all the different instruments that make up the personality keep time to the beat of one conductor.

With this rather complex map of normal language development to guide us, let's see what goes wrong when development plateaus and spurts of development occur.

Delayed language development in severe autism

In rare cases, echoing may not even develop and a child remains mute. This is indicative of severe autism. He may develop some ability to understand directions (receptive language) and follow simple commands, but expressive language (speech) remains absent. Fortunately, almost every child we have followed has eventually had a developmental spurt and has begun to talk.

It used to be said that if an autistic child did not start to talk by age five they never would begin. This is just not true. For proof, I would like to mention a friend of mine who didn't start talking till he was nine, and he hasn't stopped since. So much for that old wives' tale!

As I noted before, even if speech with words (expressive language) fails to develop, receptive language (understanding) may emerge. Take the autistic children who have never said a word but who can turn the TV to a favorite station, do complex puzzles by recognizing the shape of the pieces, take toys apart and put them back together correctly, and so on. These children are clearly not mentally retarded in the usual sense of the word, in fact they may have many skills, but just fail to develop speech.

Delayed language development in mild/high-functioning autism

The Echo Phase of language development in the normal child usually goes by so fast that only parents who are psychiatrists or linguists can catch it. However, it is common for autistic children to plateau here for weeks, months, and even (rarely) years.

When stuck in this phase they think and talk as if they had very expensive hi-fi tape recorders in their heads. This recorder can copy words, phrases, and even entire movies and television programs. It can record several people having several conversations at once. It can even copy feeling tones and accents. We had a cute little boy who had a perfect Boston accent when I interviewed him with some students, and a perfect Southern drawl after having psychological testing with Dr. B. J. Freeman, who hails from Georgia.

It is as if these kids hear something with the record button on, then, up to days or weeks later, they push the rewind button, and then the replay button. And out comes exactly what they heard. If you can imagine that you are talking to a child with such a tape recorder in his head, you must think of autism.

Not using or misusing pronouns is common in autistic children who have plateaued in this phase. This is because when they begin speaking they repeat what was last said to them. It happens this way:

"Give it to me," I say to such a child.

"Me give it to you," the child says.

"Me" was the last word he heard me say to him, and that was where he began to echo.

The same situation applies to an autistic child who refers to himself by his name, and doesn't use the pronoun "I."

"Please sing me a song, Johnny," I request.

"Johnny sings you a song," I hear back.

No pronoun was heard because he began to echo with the last word he heard, which was his name, "Johnny."

The Echo/Labeling/Concrete Phase usually lasts from one to two years in mild/high-functioning autism, and then it is gradually replaced by more advanced symbolic language as we will describe in a moment. I like to ask parents of these kids to estimate how much of what they hear from their child is echoing and how much is spontaneous. This is an interesting statistic by which to judge improvement.

In rare cases this phase lasts into the teen years, and there are even some adults who have remained plateaued here in their language ability. Thinking during this phase is very concrete. Words are only labels, and there is almost no generalization or categorization of information. In one famous experiment a bright autistic lad who was stuck in the Echo/Labeling/Concrete Phase was taught to label a milk carton and to label milk with no difficulty. But after literally thousands of teaching trials he still could not learn that milk came in milk cartons.

Because thinking in this phase is so concrete, saying symbolic things like "You just shouldn't do this or that,", or "You should be ashamed of yourself," or "Don't you want people to like you?", or "Do this to please mother," or "Do this and you will get a reward," are just like shouting into the wind. All those concepts involve symbolic meaning, not concrete things you can touch and feel. The brain of an autistic kid who is stuck in the Echo/Labeling/Concrete Phase cannot process them properly. Understanding this simple fact can save parents, loved ones, and teachers a lot of wasted time, wasted breath, and frustration. This is why these kids "just don't get it" when we use the usual teaching methods (shaming, guilt, and other typical symbolic social threats).

Some autistic children in the Echo/Labeling/Concrete Phase can show remarkable feats of memory. I recall a lad who had memorized the entire phone book of his small town. He could recite names, addresses, and phone numbers in any arrangement you asked for. There are countless instances of these kids remembering sports statistics, timetables of trains, boats, and planes, the names of capitals of states and countries, being so-called "calendar counters," and on and on. In each of these cases the parents had rewarded their child for echoing something, and their child had learned that if he repeated it he got more and more rewards. This cycle of repeating and "reinforcing" increased his desire to repeat it again and again, till he became an "expert." These kids with remarkable echoing feats are not geniuses, just experts at what they repeat over and over.

If you recall, I discussed the term *idiot savant* in chapter 1. Now you can understand how an autistic child who is stuck in the Echo/Labeling/Concrete Phase can appear gifted in a certain area. Being able to echo, having a good rote memory, and being reinforced enough can produce a child who appears very knowledgeable in a specific subject. Unfortunately, what gets memorized and echoed are words representing concrete things, and thus may have little practical value or usefulness for the child. After all, what can you do with old out-of-date train schedules, baseball statistics, and endless lists of this sort?

A classic example of echo/label/concrete thinking was portrayed in the movie *Rain Man*. The main character, a young man with mild/high-functioning autism named Raymond, was based on a composite of several autistic individuals who had been my patients. The scene I'm about to describe was filmed with humor and pathos. It opens with Raymond standing on the curb at a busy intersection. He is bright, he can read, and he has "learned" to obey street crossing signs. We see him waiting patiently till the sign flashes, WALK. He starts across the intersection, but as luck would have it he is still in the middle of the street when the sign changes to DON'T WALK. Raymond, doing what he learned to do correctly, immediately stops right in the middle of the intersection awaiting instructions to resume walking. In the movie he causes a big traffic jam and a local "redneck" gets out of his pickup with a serious case of road rage. The results are funny to watch, but sad for poor Raymond who almost gets beaten up. The fact that the sign was there to indicate danger, or meant "Hurry up and get out of the way," completely escaped Raymond. These are highly symbolic concepts. Raymond took the sign as a command. With his echo/label/concrete type of thinking WALK meant move your feet, and DON'T WALK meant stand still. Period.

One last point about language development in general needs to be stressed before we move on. We divide language into two main types. The first is called "receptive language." This is what we are able to take in, remember, and use symbolically. The second type is called "expressive language." This refers to how we communicate our thoughts via speech, writing, drawing, typing, gesticulating, etc. This distinction is important because in the Echo/Labeling/Concrete Phase of development receptive language (understanding) usually starts earlier and develops much faster than expressive language.

Delayed development of symbolic language processing in mild/ high-functioning autism and Asperger's disorder

The third and final stage of language development occurs when the parts of the brain that give symbolic meaning to words and abstract ideas mature and come online.

To explain language (cognitive) problems in this stage let's use an analogy. This time we'll compare just the language-processing parts of the brain to a big orchestra. Here's what can go wrong:

First, all the sections of the orchestra are present, but some have too many musicians and they drown out all the other sections. Second, some sections have too few musicians and they can hardly be heard at all. Third, not all the sections are playing the same tune. Fourth, and finally, not all the sections of the orchestra are following the beat of the conductor.

Now lets put this analogy to work and see how it helps us understand language-processing problems in high-functioning autism and Asperger's disorder.

First, what happens when one section drowns out the rest? The answer is simple. We get a one-dimensional, one-interest person. He uses mostly one type of thinking, and focuses on one interest all the time.

Here's an example of such a man. He is a college professor who knows all there is to know about his subject, and knows it in a rote and structured manner. While he is a well-respected international authority in his field, he has no interest in or knowledge of what his wife, his kids, and the rest of the world are like. His wife told me this:

> He is a decent man, he works hard all the time, and everybody respects him wherever he goes to teach. But outside of what he does at work, well all I can say is that he is lost, dull, and as helpless as a newborn. And he's dry. He wouldn't know a joke if it hit him on the head. All he likes to do is read and talk about what he does at school. He never had a friend because all he talks about is his subject.

This professor is a classic example of how one section (interest) can drown out all the others. His thinking is concrete and this type of thinking is busy day and night memorizing facts related to his area of interest, and replaying them in his mind over and over again. He acknowledged this to me when I asked. He is in no way bothered by it. In fact, he said he feels calmest when he is thinking about some esoteric fact in his academic field.

Then there's another middle-aged man from Los Angeles who answered my question about what he does for a living this way:

I paint. [Long pause] I paint cars. I paint the right front fender. [Longer pause, stares at the floor] I have been painting cars, the right front fender, for 35 years. [Long pause, continues to stare at the floor] And I'm good at it, and I never miss a spot. [Long pause, puts his hands in his pockets and continues to look down at the floor]

His wife went on to say:

I have to take care of everything that goes on with our life and the kids. He's there with his body, but he's never really around in a real way at all. He has always been like that, he likes to be living in his own world – but I know he loves me and I love him. He just thinks differently from us, he thinks about what he likes to do all the time.

Guess what he does in his spare time every day after work and on weekends? That's right, he paints. But what he paints at home are little HO railroad cars (model types). And yes, these little railroad cars have fascinated him since his preschool days. The visual, spatial, and color matching "sections of the orchestra of his brain" are quite normal, but they play so loudly that they drown out all other types of thinking.

Here is another example of how one type of thinking can dominate all other types. I met this fascinating man in Utah. He was hooked on organ stops. Every pipe organ has its own unique set of valves called "stops" that adjust the airflow to make different notes. Our friend traveled all over the western United States for years, and spent hours on end writing down all the various combinations of stop settings on all the pipe organs he could find. He then committed all this information to memory.

Did all this "stops" information have any useful value? None that I could think of, but when I asked him he said:

It doesn't matter that no one else thinks like me, Dr. Ritvo. I feel good when I see an organ and set its stops in my head. [Long pause] And I like to do it all the time. I can see their position and hear the music in my head and that is what I want to see and what I want to hear [pause] all the time.

Here is a final example of how one section of the orchestra (type of thinking) can drown out all the others. I had the pleasure of working with this bright teenager for many months while we got to understand his "bad habit," his type of thinking, and how he learned to live with it.

Joey, as we shall call him, was referred because he had a "bad habit." He would suddenly grab at someone's wristwatch – a teacher's, a schoolmate's, or anyone who happened to be nearby. If he got lucky and the watch came off he would rush to reset it to the "correct" time. If he happened to see a wall clock in a store or in a public place that he could get to he would make a dash for it.

As he entered adolescence his "bad habit" became more than a nuisance, and harder and harder to control. He was almost kicked out of school because of it, and security guards at the local mall had him on their watch list (pardon the pun, I couldn't resist).

His parents and I began by showing him how to ask my permission to "check and set" my watch, then theirs, and then how to ask others. Finally we took him to a watch store where he politely asked the storekeeper, and was given the greatest of rewards, the chance to reset every clock in the store.

As Joey was learning ways to be socially appropriate with his "bad habit" he started to describe the "the way I think":

> I have very "bright" thoughts and feelings when I see a watch, I see in my head that it is not set right. [Long pause] It makes me have to do something like my bad habit, I look for a "time thing" everywhere I go, I see them everywhere, and I look for them everywhere. I can see the hands and the wheels going around inside in my head.

Then with a smile he said: "I see time going by all the time in my head. I can tell you how long we have been talking, do you want to know?"

Eventually he told us he remembered that he learned how clocks work from his grandfather when he was first learning how to talk. He described how his head was always filled with "pictures" of clock faces, hands, numbers, and the wheels inside going around and around. He eventually said, without appropriate sadness, that he knew he would get into trouble if he grabbed a watch, but he couldn't stop himself.

After several months of work, Joey was able to accept the fact that he had "this kind of thinking" about watches and the wheels inside, and that he could live with his "bad habit" if he waited to set a clock in a socially acceptable manner.

I hope you can see how the four people I have just described all have plateaued in their development of symbolic language. Each has become a specialist in one type of thinking.

The first one, the professor, thinks all the time about concrete isolated facts related to his area of interest. He categorizes and re-categorizes them in his mind all day long. The second man, the painter, thinks mainly in terms of shapes and filling them with colors. The third man, Mr. Organ

Stops, thinks in pictures and sounds related to these pictures night and day. And finally, Joey constantly has pictures in his head of clock faces, wheels turning, and time frames moving by.

It is quite true that everyone, you and me included, can think just the way these four people do. But they don't think "naturally" just the way we do. For them, their "specialty" type of thinking overwhelms all their other types of thinking. They think in their "specialty" way wholesale, and can't switch it off easily. When we use their "specialty" type of thinking we do it retail, and only when we want or need to. Their brain development has plateaued midway through the symbolic phase, and they have not developed a full range of all types of thinking.

Now let's return to our analogy comparing the entire brain to a symphony orchestra. What happens when a section doesn't have enough musicians and they can hardly be heard at all?

This has occurred in almost every case of mild autism and Asperger's disorder I have ever seen. Now that's a bold statement, but I'm sure you will agree when I tell you which section of the orchestra I am referring to. It is the section that processes information about our self-image. It is the part that processes information about self-awareness, how we think about ourselves, our awareness of how other people think and feel about us and themselves, and the meaning and importance of social clues.

When you meet someone in whom this section (this type of symbolic thinking) is skimpy, and they seem "socially tuned out," a light bulb should go off in your head. You should think "autism and Asperger's disorder may live here."

I'll be discussing the issues of how these folks have difficulty relating to others in the next chapter. But remember these facts when we get there: disturbances in relatedness are caused by developmental delays in processing symbolic information.

The thinking of many people with autism or Asperger's disorder is very compartmentalized, with no connections being made between different areas of thought and no overall unity of thought. Continuing our analogy comparing the brain to an orchestra, what happens when some sections do not follow the conductor, or are not playing the same tune? Here are some case examples from my practice.

A brilliant young woman with Asperger's disorder sought my advice. She had just received a Ph.D. in linguistics from a prestigious university and was looking for a postdoctoral position in her field. While reviewing her history I asked why she had chosen to major in linguistics. This was her answer:

Because when I got to the second or third grade I found out I didn't think like the other kids. When I got to college and found out you could study about language I chose it because I thought it would help me figure out why I thought differently from everyone else I knew.

When I asked her what she meant about her thinking not being like others, she said:

Everything I think is in boxes, and I have to fight to connect the boxes. Every idea I get is separate, and I get confused and feel stupid a lot until I get it connected, but I know I'm not stupid. Once I get something I never forget it, I can see it forever. This is how I got my good grades. It was lots and lots of work, but once I got things connected I knew I knew it. When I am with friends, I have to remember that they do not think in the same way I do, I never see things connected one to the next. I can't follow conversations because I have to stop to think how one thing that someone, or even myself said, leads to the next ... I wanted learning linguistics to show me how everyone else thinks, even in different languages. They were hard to learn like everything else ... When I read about Asperger's knew I was like them because I don't need friends and I don't understand people, like they don't. But I have to ask you – do you know other people who think like me, who think in boxes?

Another young woman with Asperger's disorder told me that when she enters a room she is immediately aware of its shape and volume.

I can easily and exactly recall the colors of wallpaper, rugs, and curtains. I can tell exactly how high the ceiling is and how long the walls are. The volume of a room is important to me. The volume has to be right for the room and I can tell right off if it's OK or not. If it is not, I want to leave.

I asked her what happens if there are people in a room when she walks in.

Probably I don't even see them, and if I do I can only recall what color clothes they had on, and never what they looked like, or what their names were.

Her world contains shapes, objects, and spaces, and registers a myriad of colors. Other aspects may be recalled, but they hold little interest.

Another very common complaint from these people is that they cannot connect their own gestures to what they are saying. The other side of this is just as confusing, trying to figure our what other people's gestures mean.

One young man confessed that he couldn't tell from someone's tone of voice how that person was feeling, just as he couldn't tell what his own tone of voice meant. The content and the feelings were not automatically symbolically connected. He "confessed" with much difficulty that he had to "learn" to "read" feelings when he got to high school so he wouldn't "look stupid" to the other kids and his teachers.

Some patients have told me that they think in only black-and-white pictures. Some only see words in their mind. And some complain that they can only focus on one subject at a time, and get very upset when their thoughts are interrupted.

Jokes and analogies are hard to deal with because of their highly symbolic nature. Many jokes are funny because you have to connect things in your mind that usually are not connected. If you have concrete thinking and trouble with catching on to subtle symbolic meanings, you will keep missing the point of such jokes. Puns, sarcasm, and hostile humor are equally difficult for the same reason.

As I mentioned before, one of the most common problems resulting from the failure to develop symbolic thinking fully is a lack of self-awareness. This is why almost all people with mild autism and Asperger's disorder do not think of themselves as odd or different till they reach the preteen years. This is the age they first are told by their peers that they are "odd balls," "weirdos," and other such teenage terms. It is something they have to be told, it does not come spontaneously or from natural self-awareness.

Contrast this lack of self-awareness with shy and awkward early teenagers. They're usually full of anxieties because they "aren't cool," "don't fit in," "aren't wearing the right clothes," or are "not in a 'cool' group at school," and so on, day after day. They live on a distant planet from the mild autistic and Asperger's teenager who is "socially tuned out" or "socially blind."

A final example of disconnected or compartmentalized thinking at this stage is seen in those who are unable to classify information in the usual sense. We have worked with many who think only in pictures. Others tell us they need to have everything written down to understand it completely. In these people the sections of the brain that process images and writing are overused.

Delayed development of relatedness

Here are the milestones we look for along the road of normal development of the capacity to relate:

1. First, an infant smiles at faces, beginning about eight weeks of age (the "smiling response").

2. Next, at about eight months we can see anxiety when unfamiliar people come into view ("stranger anxiety").

3. Next, symbolic language processing emerges. From here on the capacity to relate goes hand in hand with symbolic language development. As the brain develops this ability words relating to people and objects become more and more sophisticated. Unique and specific attachment to parents, caretakers, and toys are made. The teddy bear that comforts is called a "security object" because of its symbolic connection with mother or father; seeing it "reminds" baby of her mother.

4. Finally, social customs, ritualistic interpersonal interactions (chitchat like "Hi, how are you?," "How are you feeling?," "How's it going?") and appropriate gestures all come online. At this point children can understand the "golden rule" of "do unto others—," and how to get approval or punishment from their parents, as the case may be. They become socially "tuned in," develop self-awareness ("theory of the mind," as I discussed before), and are concerned about what others think about them.

Now lets see what goes awry in autism and Asperger's disorder as the degree of severity of the condition increases.

Delayed relatedness in severe autism

These are the children who don't even get off the launching pad. They fail to show the smiling response at eight weeks of age, or lose this ability soon after. They are the "early onset" cases we talked about before. They can be said to be truly "autistic" in the sense that Dr. Bleuler first coined the term; they simply do not develop the capacity to relate to others. Fortunately, the vast majority of infants who plateau at this stage have developmental spurts during the next one or two years and move on to further stages of relating.

Children stuck at this phase treat people as objects. They throw toys with no regard for hitting someone, and parents are hit and pinched with no awareness that they are causing pain or injury. They will injure themselves inadvertently as well. And they frequently will go to dangerous places that require heroic rescue efforts. Climbing on top of walls, furniture, roofs, and other risky places are all commonly seen. Constant supervision is the watchword for the caretakers of these fearless kids, as they have no awareness of what we consider dangerous.

As I just pointed out, fortunately the vast majority of autistic children have developmental spurts and progress beyond this very early stage.

Delayed relatedness in mild/high-functioning autism

Here rote memory, echoing, and other intellectual functions like singing, drawing, and copying actions develop. However, the parts of the brain that give symbolic meaning to people and objects fail to develop fully as we described in the language-delay section above. Their thinking remains primarily of the echo/labeling/concrete type.

While parents and others can have special meaning at this stage, they still may be treated as objects. People are not grouped as friends, foes, strangers, pals, or what have you. Those are highly symbolic categories.

Toys are used in a special way. The child, not the toy maker, determines their purpose. A toy train is not a train; it is a little square block of wood with round things that spin, labeled wheels. Mother is something with smooth hair to rub, with shiny jewelry to stare at, and has a nose to pinch. In short, she is an object that provides an endless source of delightful sensory stimuli.

It used to be said that autistic children stuck at this level of relatedness avoid eye contact. We now know that is about as silly as saying deaf children avoid hearing or that blind children avoid seeing. No, autistic children do not seek or attend to eye contact simply because it has no special meaning for them. Since they are not able to give symbolic meaning to "the look in mother's eye," or need to look at her face to see if it registers approval, love, or anger, why should they look?

As developmental spurts occur in the language-processing area of their brain, these children develop more normal ways of relating to their parents and objects. Becoming very attached to mother, father, a sister or brother, a caretaker, or a teacher may "suddenly" start at age three to six for example. When this happens, changing from one place to another, or going from the care of one person to another, becomes very difficult and can lead to major tantrums. At this stage we say they have difficulty "making transitions."

When a child needs to be with one special person all the time in order to be comfortable, we say that child is in the "symbiotic phase" of relating. These kids need special care to help them learn to be comfortable when alone or with strangers.

This is also the stage when teaching socially appropriate behavior should begin. More about that later when we get to treatment, but suffice it to say that socially appropriate behavior can only be learned when the brain has developed to a point where simple symbolic processing is possible. Before that time, you are just wasting your breath trying to teach appropriate ways of relating.

Disturbed relatedness in high-functioning autism and Asperger's disorder

Everyone with high-functioning autism and Asperger's disorder has difficulty in relating to others and feeling comfortable in groups because of their difficulty in understanding the symbolic meaning of social cues. This is a major hallmark of their disorder. It is what gets them called "odd ducks," "loners," "social misfits," "hermits," "recluses," "schizoid," "antisocial," and a host of other more derogatory terms.

Sadly, more often than not, they become the object of prejudice. This tends to reinforce their desire to remain alone, and a vicious cycle of increasing desire for more isolation takes place. Unfortunately, we have seen this vicious cycle devastate the lives of many of our patients, both young and old. But we have also seen many who have formed long-term relationships with spouses, their children, and friends. In these cases their partners have accepted their social-relatedness problems and compensated for them.

I remember with a smile now something that brought tears of frustration several years ago. It was in 1988, and I was trying to publish the first paper describing autistic parents. This research will be described in some detail in chapter 5 when we talk about our family studies and genetics. But the point here is that in 1988 no one believed that autistic children could grow up, get married, and have kids. We got six rejection letters from six of the most respected scientific journals. Their wise and all-knowing reviewers "just knew" it couldn't happen, and we were crazy even to suggest it. The seventh journal's reviewers took a gamble on us; and, of course, today everyone accepts the fact that adults with mild autism can marry and have children.

I'll describe in detail several parents with autism and Asperger's disorder in chapter 7 ("My Casebook"). As you will see, in their families the non-affected parents do most of the business and parenting. The affected parents relate in an aloof and stilted fashion. A great example of this occurred when I was interviewing the mother of an autistic boy who was married to a high-functioning autistic man. I asked (being a well-trained Freudian psychoanalyst):

"You have three children, tell me, how did your husband learn about the birds and the bees?"

She answered me very quickly, very directly, and very sincerely:

"He learned what he had to do, and he did it."

Her answer gives you a glimpse of the mechanical, non-feeling, detached world in which her husband lives. No bouquet of roses, no "some enchanted evening," no flirting, no subtle seduction. No, they were not for him. Referring to the most intimate act a married couple can share, he simply "learned what he had to do, and he did it."

An example of echo/concrete non-symbolic thinking comes from a videotape made by one of my friends at UCLA, Professor James Q. Simmons III. Jim, as we call him, was interviewing a teenage mildly autistic boy with a Fellow in Child Psychiatry. The results were so classic that we gave Jim an Oscar, and used the tape for many years in our classes. Here's how it went:

Jim: "Hi Frankie, how are you doing today?"

Frank: "Hi, I am talking to you today." [A concrete answer he says in a flat monotone nasal voice that does not change in tone or volume throughout the tape.]

Jim: "Thank you for coming to my office. Is it OK if we ask you some questions?"

Frank: "Yes it is OK if you ask me some questions."

Jim: "Will you tell us, Frank, do you have a girlfriend?"

Frank: "Yes, I will tell you, I do have a girlfriend."

Jim: "Will you tell us about your girlfriend, what's she like?"

Frank: "Yes I will tell you about my girlfriend, this is what she is like. When I go to the movies she has a flashlight and she shows me to my seat. She is a girl and she is very friendly, so she is my girlfriend."

Jim: "Do you know her name, Frankie?"

Frank: "No, I do not need to know her name. She is my girlfriend without me needing to know her name."

Jim: "That's very interesting. Now tell me, Frankie, do you like to read Playboy magazine?"

Frank: "Yes, I like to read Playboy magazine."

Jim: "When do you read it?"

Frank: "I read it when it is there."

Jim: "Tell us, what do you think of the centerfold girls?"

Frank: "It is not nice to dress naked."

I trust you can easily see why I said this was a classic example of echo/concrete non-symbolic thinking. This mild/high-functioning autistic teenager has a girl who is a friend, whom he concretely translates into being a "girlfriend." Does he "really" have a "girlfriend," a "girl of his dreams"? No, not by my standards when I was his age. And how do you explain "naked" as a way of being dressed?

Try to imagine what your life would be like if you saw the world as Frankie does. How would his type of thinking shape your relationships and the way you got along in life?

To sum up, delayed relatedness is one of the main hallmarks of high-functioning autism and Asperger's disorder. When you encounter someone who thinks this way, you must think of autism or Asperger's disorder!

Autism and intelligence

Before leaving the subject of clinical symptoms I want to touch briefly on the issue of intellectual endowment and "mental retardation" in relation to autism and Asperger's disorder.

Let me confess right now that if you gave me an IQ test in Russian, Greek, or Japanese you could easily "prove" that I had a very low IQ and was "mentally retarded." Obviously (I hope) you realize that since I don't speak these languages I couldn't answer the test question correctly, even if I knew the answers. The tests were not designed to take into account my handicap, namely, I only speak English.

This simple mistake was overlooked years ago when autistic kids were first given IQ tests that were developed for non-autistic children. Regular IQ tests are standardized on kids who have normal language-processing skills, and autistic kids obviously have developmental delays in language processing. Naturally then, they did poorly. This is how word spread around that "autistic kids are mentally retarded" and that autism was a "type of mental retardation." Believe it or not, this myth is still believed even today by many who should know better.

Let me give you the bottom line right here on my thinking regarding IQ and autism. When teaching my advanced postdoctoral classes I use the complex scientific formulation called "marble theory" to explain this complicated problem. It states:

> Children with autism and Asperger's disorder are born with the same number of "marbles" (or IQ points) as everyone else. Having autism affects only their ability to use their "marbles," not how many God gave them to begin with.

In less fancy words, autism and Asperger's disorder on one hand, and IQ on the other, are independent of each other. Some of my patients have a very high IQ, the vast majority are in the average range, and some are low.

Dr. B.J. Freeman, a professor of medical psychology at UCLA, and a key member of our research team, showed this several years ago. First she adapted IQ tests to fit each autistic child she tested. She did this to compensate for their language delays, just as she would have had to adjust her tests for blind or deaf children.

The first time she tested the kids she found some tested high, some low, and most were in the middle, as she had expected. She then retested the same children year after year for over a decade. The results showed that the IQ scores did not change as the children grew up and became teenagers and young adults. Not one single child showed a significant drop in IQ. This is one piece of good news we hasten to give all the parents of our young autistic patients.

Chapter 3

The Life Course of Autism and Asperger's Disorder

Every time I have the painful responsibility of making the diagnosis of autism or Asperger's disorder questions like these come up:

- What will he (or she) be like when he grows up?

- Will he outgrow it?

- Will he be cured if we act now?

- Will he be able to go to a regular school?

- Will he be able to graduate from college?

- Will he be able to hold a job and make a living?

- Will he be able to get married and have children?

- Will he get epilepsy?

- Will he live to be old?

- Will he be mentally retarded?

- Will this affect our other kids?

- Are you sure? Dr. X said he does not have it.

- Will he be— (and a thousand other questions)?

These are just a few of the questions that plague every parent when they first learn their child has autism or Asperger's disorder. And they want answers, and they deserve answers.

Unfortunately, the first thing I have to share with parents when we start talking about the future is that there are no hard facts on which I, or anyone for that matter, can base predictions. However, I can and do give them my "best guesses" based on my four decades of experience at UCLA watching hundreds of kids grow from early childhood to adulthood.

But before I give them my "best guesses" I have to confess that they aren't all that good. Many long years ago I wisely gave up trying to predict what the school years and adulthood would bring for my own seven children, my friends' kids, and my little non-autistic patients. And for children with an autism and Asperger's disorder the future is even more difficult to predict because there's a "joker" in the deck.

In autism and Asperger's disorder that "joker," that "big unknown," is how much brain development is yet to come, as a child grows older. Given lots of love, family support, and the benefits of appropriate supportive treatments, each child's prognosis (and eventual outcome) is mainly determined by this crucial factor. Since the vast majority of these children continue to have spurts of brain growth up until their late teen years, and in some cases until their early twenties, I always remain optimistic!

Given all these reservations, here are my "best guesses." I have prepared a chart that I hope will make thing a little clearer (Table 1). It summarizes the life course of those with severe autism, mild/high-functioning autism, and Asperger's disorder.

The life course of severe autism

This is the most serious form of autism. These are like the children Kanner first described, the ones who became the templates for diagnosing autism from the 1940s to the 1970s, before we discovered the mild forms and Asperger's disorder. Fortunately this form of autism is very rare, and comprises only about 5–10 percent of all the cases I have seen.

These children have developmental delays from the first months of life or plateau at about age two. They may fail to develop useful expressive language. Their receptive language usually outpaces their expressive language, but even this remains poor. They echo at best, with little useful verbal communication, sometimes learning to use picture books, pointing, pulling an adult by the hand, and other non-verbal means. They do not develop specific attachments to their parents or others, and they treat people and

Table 1 The life course of autism and Asperger's disorders

	Severe autism	Mild/high-functioning autism	Asperger's and subclinical type
Age first seen, and developmental course	Early or late onset type, few plateaus and spurts seen, major separation of development pathways	Usually during preschool years, plateaus and spurts till adulthood, separation of pathways early in life, teens hard	Usually first noted in elementary school or early teens, subclinical, not seen by doctors
Sensory-motor symptoms	Over and underreactions to sensations (perceptual inconstancy), resistance to changes remains lifelong	Same as severe, but may disappear by adolescence, isolated ones may remain lifelong, routines, special interests and rituals remain	May be clumsy, need routines, repetitive actions, and unique interests
Symptoms relating to people and objects	Aloof, do not use eye contact, may become symbiotic for a while, no appropriate interpersonal affect, no bonding to others, fixates on objects	Obvious social deficits lifelong, maintain immature patterns of relating, use objects in unique ways, no true friends	"Socially blind," misread social cues, lack friends, "odd ducks," little or no empathy
Speech, language, cognition symptoms	Mute or speech lost, rote/concrete thinking, atonal, can't measure IQ	Echo/concrete, some useable language, perseverative interests, poor symbolic use	No general delay, pedantic and special types of thinking, no imagination, special interests
Level of social functioning	Lifelong family or professional supervision with protected living environment required	Support at home when young and then community-based programs may be needed, no close friends, can be bar mitzvah or confirmed, etc., may hold a job	Awkward, bullied at school, may marry but dependent on spouse. mechanical distant type relationships
Educational and occupational level	Lifelong, behavioral based programs needed	Need IEP, may finish high school and college; with vocational help, many jobs can be learned	May finish professional training, usually self-supporting in adulthood, repetitive work
Medical follow-up requirements	Frequent, signs of other diseases may not be noted	Counseling and social skills "coaching" help	Daily living and social skills "coaching"

objects alike. They have sensory-motor symptoms (flapping, twirling, perceptual inconstancy, body rocking, staring at spinning objects, making repetitive sounds, etc.) that may persist into adulthood. They frequently display isolated skills, such as being able to take apart and put together complicated things like toasters and record players, learning directions when taken places, drawing, and doing jigsaw puzzles by aligning the shape of the pieces. These are called "splinter skills," and their presence lets us know that they are not simply "mentally retarded." Rather it proves that they have the uneven brain development that I described previously as a hallmark of autism.

As these kids grow older, strong spurts of development are unfortunately not seen. The marked separation of the three developmental pathways, sensory-motor, language, and relatedness, persist as they get older.

These children show little or no response to our supportive treatments. They may master simple repetitive tasks, but even these may require frequent reinforcement. They require continual supervision and behavior-management controls.

Adolescence is a particularly difficult time for them, and brief periods of residential placement with round-the-clock professional supervision may be required. For example, this happens when puberty leads to aggressiveness, or if they simply grow too big to be managed at home by their elderly or infirm parents. Or it may be necessary if they display socially inappropriate behavior, such as masturbation in public places. Consider this: it's no "big deal" if a five-year-old boy takes his pants down and waves his penis around in the mall. An embarrassed mother can quickly isolate him from prying or shocked eyes, and quickly and quietly zip up his fly. As I said, that's "no big deal." But it's quite a different "deal" if you are dealing with a six-foot 19-year-old "boy" who weighs 190 pounds, mostly muscle, who does the same thing in a shopping mall!

In rare circumstances I have used short-term sedative-type medications to control dangerous behaviors in adolescents. I like to start this type of treatment in my hospital and then continue it for a few months on an out-patient basis. I shall discuss the use of medications in chapter 6.

During the late adolescent years lifelong living arrangements need to be considered. Community-based state and privately financed group homes and apartments are available in almost every major city I have visited in the United States and abroad. They are needed whenever parents are no longer able to provide adequate supervision, or one or both die.

Life estate planning is also essential as adults with severe autism can and do live long physically healthy lives. Fortunately there are lawyers who specialize in working with families of developmentally disabled persons in need of estate planning. They can easily be located by contacting a local legal association.

Before leaving this subject I want to say again that I always remain optimistic, even about the most serious cases, like the ones I'm describing here. Here are two examples of severely autistic kids whose life course defied prediction when they were young.

The first is a boy who fooled us all by not talking until he was eleven years old. Now he is in his mid-thirties and lives at home with his parents. He eats them out of house and home, as we say, he is usually quite cheerful, and loves video games. He has a job that is supervised by a vocational rehabilitation counselor and goes bowling once a week. And here is the punchline: now he only stops talking when he's asleep.

Another girl with severe autism I recall surprised her parents when she began to speak and learned to read at age seven. Her thinking then plateaued at the echo/labeling/concrete stage, but her sensory-motor symptoms abated and she learned to relate in a stilted and shy manner. She completed a high school special education course with much mainstreaming during which peer tutors helped her improve her social skills. She also learned to play the piano and to sing beautifully. She enjoyed giving concerts at school and at the Autism Society's annual meetings. Now, in her early twenties, she lives in a "supervised" apartment with an autistic roommate and goes to a sheltered workshop program each day. She loves to go shopping with her salary and buys CDs. Unlike her old records, these don't wear out, and she is quite skilled at operating the CD player that her parents have yet to master. She is emotionally close to her family, her language is still quite concrete, but she has almost no echoing or sensory-motor symptoms left.

Finally, here is an obvious caveat about living with a severely autistic person. It is vital to have frequent medical checkups for those who can't communicate well with words. Any sudden change in behavior or regression should make you think that they could be physically sick. Since they are not able to tell you in the usual way when something hurts, you have to be a real Sherlock Holmes when it comes to monitoring their health.

The life course of mild/high-functioning autism

Here is where the surprises come (pleasant surprises that is), and predictions are particularly perilous. I never make any "guesses" or even tentative predictions about the future of these kids until they are at least in their early teens. To do so before they are that old does them an injustice. And I always dismiss right off the bat any earlier predictions a family has been given by others. As I pointed out at the beginning of this chapter, and want to stress again at the risk of being boring, spurts of brain development can and do occur up until the early twenties. Because of this fact it is simply impossible to know what a child's ultimate developmental level will be until that many birthdays have gone by.

Here is more good news. I have never seen a child with mild/high-functioning autism lose thinking abilities (cognitive functions), regress in their ability to relate to others, or develop new sensory-motor symptoms after age five or six. While progress is slow during a plateau phase, worsening (regression) does not occur.

These children are subject to social pressures and can develop emotional problems just as non-autistic children can. Depression, anxiety attacks, phobias, obsessions and compulsions, and even more severe reactions are rarely seen. But in my experience, they do not occur more frequently in autistic kids than non-autistic kids, and do not occur just because they have autism.

An important emotional hurdle always comes when a child learns that he or she has autism. (This usually causes more concern in the parents than the child.) No matter how sheltered they may have been from hearing the "A" word, these kids always ask about it sooner or later. The best approach I have learned over the years is to keep the word autism out of the family vocabulary till the child is at least five or six. I also recommend waiting for the child to first ask about autism, and then be quite frank with simple answers. By no means overdo it with lengthy explanations and lectures, and so on. For a five- to ten-year-old here is what is usually sufficient:

> Yes, you do have autism. Yes, it is a disorder that makes it hard for you to understand how some other people think and feel about things. No, it won't kill you. No, your habits won't hurt you. No, your sister does not have it. Yes, this is why you are in a special education class. No, this is not why your brother could go on sleep-over when he was eight and you can't. Why can't you? Just because I said so. Yes, you will get better from it as you get older. And yes, you can have music lessons and join the band some day at school when you are older. And yes, you can have karate lessons. Now stop with all the questions. We'll have time for more later. Now it's time for supper, so go and wash up.

When parents ask: "Will my child outgrow it, will he look normal, will he be able to blend into society so no one ever will ever know he had mild autism?" I give this answer: "I don't know." All our predictions of long-term outcome are thrown off by the fact that those with mild autism and Asperger's disorder who improve to the point where they can live "normal" lives don't come in to be counted. They live in society as "subclinical" cases. The only way to find out how many such subclinical cases there are would be to follow thousands of such young kids into adulthood. Since no one would fund such a long-term follow-up study, the answer will forever remain a mystery.

To illustrate this problem, just think about the autistic *parents* (that's parents, not patients) we first identified in the 1980s. We had tons of trouble just convincing others that they even existed. (They will be described in detail in later chapters.) We found them only because they had autistic children who were in our research studies, not because they thought they were sick or had been previously identified as having autism. How many other parents like them are out there in the world? Your guess is as good as mine.

Let's go back to the questions I listed at the beginning of this chapter. Here are typical answers I will give to parents of a preschool child I have just diagnosed as having mild/high-functioning autism.

- "Could you be wrong?" I am often asked. — Yes, especially if the child is less than three years old and I have made only a tentative diagnosis.

- "What will he (or she) be like when he grows up?" — No one can tell you this before the teen years, and if someone does try to tell you, simply smile and politely walk away. You can't educate such "experts."

- "Will he outgrow it?" — No one can tell because very mild cases fade from our clinical view and live "normal lives." They are then called "subclinical." How many are like this, no one knows.

- "Will he be able to go to a regular school?" — Yes, it is usually best and almost always possible for children with mild/high-functioning autism to attend regular schools in special educational classrooms. I also recommend that they spend as much time in regular classes as they can. This is called "mainstreaming." There are, however, special circumstances when I recommend a school that is just for developmentally delayed children.

- "Will he be able to graduate from college?" — This depends on the severity of his symptoms when he gets to college age. Many of my mild/high-functioning autistic kids have gone on to college. They had received the usual family support, it was what they had wanted, and they had been willing to work hard for it. Most colleges today are very cooperative when it comes to assisting developmentally disabled students. You will find that many even have special personnel dedicated to helping developmentally delayed students. Parents should check this out ahead of time, and don't apply to a college that won't take into account your child's special needs, whatever they may be.

- "Will he be able to hold a job and make a living?" — Almost all those with mild/high-functioning autism can be employed, in keeping with the severity of their symptoms in adulthood. Vocational training and professional training are crucial in this regard. Let me tell you that the best cab driver in Washington, DC is a young man with typical high-function autism. He knows every street in the city, the shortest, quickest and safest way to get there, never bothers his passengers with chitchat conversation, and always gives the exact amount of change. I have patients who have jobs such as cashiers, food servers, ticket takers, ushers, and store clerks, despite having obvious but mild symptoms. Jobs that require repetitive activities that would bore some others to death are often just what they like. Farm work is ideal as it usually follows a set routine day after day, season after season. Book keeping and other clerical jobs suit those with these cognitive skills.

- "Will he be able to get married and have children?" — Yes, again in keeping with the severity of his symptoms when he reaches adulthood. Several of the autistic parents we first identified had typical mid/high-functioning autism, and had never been diagnosed.

- "Will he get epilepsy?" — No, this is very, very, very rare, despite earlier reports.

- "Will he live to be old?" — Yes, these disorders do not shorten the lifespan.

- "Will he be mentally retarded?" — Mental retardation and autism are not directly related. Once language develops beyond the echo/concrete stage the IQ remains stable and is "normally distributed" as in the general population.

- "Will this affect our other kids?" — Not in a negative way. Most non-autistic brothers and sisters I know have turned out to be more generous of spirit, more kind, more mature, and more empathetic when they reach the teen years and adulthood. They learn early that life is not always "fair" and that they are the lucky ones. They know that "it is more blessed to give than to receive."

- "Will he be more likely to have other illnesses, like allergies?" — No, he will be just as likely to have any other illness as anyone else. These kids have the same number of allergies, infections, and other illnesses as their non-autistic brothers and sisters and the general public.

- "Will this cost us a fortune, which we don't have, and will insurance cover it?" — No, it should not cost you anything extra. If you are based in the USA, your Regional Center and school district will cover the cost of special education and the supportive treatments I recommend. *Autism spectrum disorders are considered medical conditions and are covered by insurance companies, unless your policy specifically excludes them by name.* Outside the USA, please check with your local Autism Society to find out what provisions are available in your country of residence.

I fought for autism to be considered a medical condition by insurance companies some years ago with the help of the father of one of my patients with autism. His insurance company turned down his son's UCLA bill saying autism was a "mental disease" and thus was not covered as a physical disease would be. We sued this insurance company in the Federal District Court here in Los Angeles. We won the case and it was upheld on appeal. This made it almost a "law," and forced all insurance companies to pay for autism as a physical (neurological) disease, not as a mental or emotional disease as they had been doing. The name in the federal register of cases is the "Kunin case." If your insurance company turns you down saying autism or Asperger's disorder is excluded from coverage because it is a psychiatric or mental condition, cite the Kunin case in your appeal, or have your lawyer do so. They will wake up fast, as they can be subject to severe penalties if they wrongfully deny you insurance cover.

The life course of Asperger's disorder

I'm treading on very thin ice when I discuss this subject. Since this form of autistic spectrum disorder was only recognized a few years ago, we have not had enough time to conduct any long-term follow-up studies. Thus most of what we know comes from watching our young patients and from adults re-calling their childhood memories.

The most common thing I hear from little kids is that they want to be "left alone" to do what they want, and playing with other kids in not what they want to do.

> I don't want to play with other kids at all, I don't want to go to school and be with the other kids, I want to stay and play in my room, I don't know why the other kids don't like me, I want to do what I want to do and don't care what they want to do, I don't care if they don't like me, I want to read what I want to read and not that stuff. I hate the soccer team, I hate "T" ball, and I hate to go to school.

These are not social phobias, or expressions of anxiety or rebelliousness. No, these kids just "don't get it" in terms of what other kids expect of them when they play together. They are thinking what they are thinking, and don't want to be bothered by having to think about what other kids want them to think about.

I recall very clearly a nine-year-old boy to whom I gave a "curbstone diagnosis" of Asperger's disorder. He was on my son's flag football team, which I was coaching. During tryouts I tossed a ball to him while I thought he was looking at me. It hit him on the chest. After the next one hit him on his nose I asked him what was going on. Here is what he said in a flat, nasal, atonal, expressionless voice that raised my index of suspicion:

> I don't care what you are doing or throwing at me, I am here because my father made me, and I am not going to think about stupid football because I don't care about stupid football, even though my father does, so I don't care about what you think, and I don't like to get hit with the stupid football anyway. Please, leave me alone.

By coincidence his school counselor referred him to me for an evaluation because he "didn't fit in." He was doing well academically, but had no friends, couldn't relate appropriately to his teachers, and was starting to be picked on by the other kids. Was he was surprised when he found out that "Coach Ed" was also a doctor! I had little trouble making the diagnosis of Asperger's disorder. He was a brilliant student, by far the smartest kid in his class at a very competitive private school. But his social skills were at a kin-dergarten level, and he couldn't care less what the other kids and the teach-ers thought of him. He spent his time thinking about chess moves he could see in his head, and classical music he played in his head, and other things that he "liked to think about." He wanted to be a "good boy" but had no clue as to how others saw him or how to be "one of the boys."

He did very well over the next year. I met with him individually and went with him and his parents for "social coaching" sessions. He transferred to a different private school that was staffed with patient teachers and we built "social skills training" into his curriculum. He took up karate, a sport where he competed only against himself, and had no other kids depending on him to catch a ball who were ready to laugh at him if he dropped it.

Adolescence is usually the hardest time in life for kids with Asperger's disorder. These are the years when the social pressures to conform with their peers are the greatest, when they struggle with puberty, and when the need to become independent arises. This is when emotional problems are most likely to surface, because they cannot adapt their thinking style to fit in, and they become aware that they are "socially blind." They most often become increasingly socially isolated and the "loner" label gets stuck on them.

In many cases I know of these children have found intellectual interests that prove to be roads to success in high school and college. One girl I recall well took up art and dancing in high school and majored in these subjects at college. Another young man I know was interested in Native Americans in high school and received a scholarship in this field when he applied to college. He is now a professor in a very prestigious university, a recognized expert in a related field.

As I discussed before, I know many married adults with Asperger's disorder who have children. Some have sought marriage counseling. In the majority of cases the spouse complaining and seeking treatment was the non-Asperger's one. The one with Asperger's disorder is usually not aware of the anguish their need for social isolation produces in their spouse. On the contrary, they view the marriage as a shelter from the world of confusing social cues and social responsibilities.

Recently, due to increased public awareness, I have received many requests from adults wondering whether they have Asperger's disorder. Some thought of this themselves after reading a book or something on the internet. Others had it suggested to them by someone else, usually a husband or wife. In the majority of those whom I have found do indeed have it (only a small percentage of all those who have asked) their major complaints go something like this:

> I know I don't think like other people. What is important to me is different from what's important to others. I knew when I was young

that I just couldn't get along with other kids so I didn't try, I just never wanted to have friends, I was always better off doing what interested me. I had no troubled in school because I could memorize things, I think better by myself, I can only work on a job where I am alone.

When I questioned parents, brothers and sisters, and friends of these same people I got these comments:

- He was a loner from his early years on up.

- She never had friends, went out to play, or seemed interested in what the other kids were doing.

- He was an "odd duck" from the time he was in grammar school.

- He was always doing a peculiar special thing like collecting something or studying something silly, and he never showed much affection or real concern.

- She seemed to be like a robot at times and at other times not.

- He was so fussy about his clothes and being on time that he was rude about it.

- She was always messy and never on time to the point of being rude.

- He just didn't tune in to what others in the family were doing or thought important.

- She would get lost in a world of her own weird interests sometimes and ignore things like meals.

- He only got angry if we interfered with his "habits" or his "routines."

- He never showed any physical affection and he never wanted to be hugged or touched.

- He was a "good dad" but not an affectionate one.

- He needed to be looked after like one of the kids most of the time.

- He "tuned out" sometimes for hours when he got interested in something and you couldn't get his attention.

And of all the comments, by far the most common goes like this:

> He just doesn't think like the rest of us. Some things we say don't get across, he seems most happy when we leave him alone to do what he wants to do, and he just doesn't seem to tune in to other people.

Again I must stress that there is no way to tell how many, or what percentage of those with Asperger's disorder are out there making it successfully in the world. I have run into many people who obviously to me have Asperger's disorder, but are totally unaware of it. And, rest assured, I would never mention it to them. They include doctors, lawyers, housewives and businessmen. In fact, I have used some of their services professionally. In other words, Asperger's disorder is completely compatible with successful independent living.

Over the past several years many adults have consulted me to find out if they had high-functioning autism or Asperger's disorder. Without exception, every time this proved to be the diagnosis the person was most grateful. They knew they were "different somehow" and were relieved finally to be able to give it a name. They said that it was easier to cope with their problems once I explained why they had unique ways of thinking, difficulty reading social cues, and relationship problems. Many were comforted to learn that they were not the only one in the world with similar problems. And most important, many sought appropriate counseling or coaching, individually or in support groups. It was most gratifying to hear later how this had changed their lives for the better. In a few cases prior misdiagnoses had led to unnecessary drug treatments that not only had not helped, but also caused worrisome side effects. With their new proper diagnosis and self-awareness they were able to prevent such tragedies from recurring.

Having the proper diagnosis has been just as beneficial for the loved ones of those who had not been properly diagnosed before. Most had no understanding of why their loved ones thought the way they did and acted in "such strange ways." Many had been frustrated by misdiagnoses that had led to more confusion and useless treatments that simply wasted their time and money. Many of them had understandably "just got fed up" with what they considered uncaring, unempathetic, and selfish traits in their loved ones. I was told many times that just getting the proper diagnosis and an explanation that it was not their loved one's "fault" allowed compassion to replace frustration and anger. As the old saying goes, "knowledge is power."

Chapter 4

Searching the Brain
for Clues

Following our medical model of disease, we now can ask ourselves: "What goes wrong in the brain that causes developmental delays and the clinical symptoms?" To answer this I'll guide you down the winding and branching research trail that we've been following since 1963. But before we start I want to share some of the fascinating things that made this long journey possible.

First of all, I have been blessed with a large group of patients and their families ready, willing, and able to support our research. No matter how crazy our ideas seemed, or what discomforts they involved, once we explained what we needed there were always plenty of volunteers. And without their help we would still be right where we started.

Second, all of our research required the collaboration of other scientists, each with special knowledge and special tools. Emphasis here is on the word "required." The day of the lone investigator working away by himself is long gone in our technically sophisticated world. While we had the patients, others had the tools, and progress only came with cooperation.

Third, I was lucky to have been working during exciting decades of rapid scientific progress. I was "hanging ten" on the crest of waves of new discoveries, as my surfer friends would say. It's hard to imagine, but most of the special tools and techniques we used to study autism hadn't been invented when I started. For example, in the 1960s we didn't even know that nerve cells talked to one another by sending out chemical messengers, there were no CAT (computed axial tomography), MRI (magnetic resonance imaging) or PET (positron emission tomography) scans, and no one had even dreamed of DNA (deoxyribonucleic acid) and RNA (ribonucleic acid), the chemical instructions in our genes.

Fourth, I was lucky enough to have found three parents of our autistic patients who joined our research team. They contributed original ideas and worked countless days, nights, and weekends. And their only reward was knowing that they had contributed to the understanding of their child's disease. We are proud to have placed their names in our scientific articles, and you will meet them in person when we discuss their contributions.

Also on the list of collaborators who made our work possible are about two dozen "slave laborers." In the medical school world we affectionately call students who volunteer to work on research projects "slaves." That's because they work inhuman hours for meager rewards, such as letters of recommendation or co-authorship on research publications in obscure scientific journals. That's exactly how I started out in college, as a "slave laborer," cleaning the autopsy room floor at Boston City Hospital. Without such dedicated efforts from our students we would still be back in the Dark Ages.

A model to guide the search for abnormal brain development

We needed a theoretical model, a map, of how the brain works to guide our research efforts. We chose one that compares the brain to a computer (Figure 3).

By the way, when we started in the 1960s computers were not little magic black boxes that sat on you lap like a poodle, like the one I'm writing on now. No, they were two-ton steel "mainframe" monsters that lived in basements of universities. They breathed only air-conditioned, temperature-controlled, dehumidified air. Specially trained nerds who wore white coats and spoke in strange languages such as COBOL fed them information. They kept us waiting days, not seconds, for results. And when we finally got results they were printed in strange codes on miles of folded paper with little holes on the sides. Reading those results took another lifetime.

But putting our love–hate relationship with computers aside, they provide a good model for how the brain is organized. As Figure 3 shows, we divided our model of the brain into three main parts: (1) input systems, (2) central processing unit, and (3) output systems.

In the computer the input systems represent our senses (hearing, seeing, feeling, tasting, smelling, and temperature and position sense). The information processing part (the central processing unit or CPU in "com-

A Computer

Input Systems	Central Processing Unit	Output Systems
Keyboard	Processing Chips	Speakers
Scanner	Software	Fax
Camera	Memory, Modem	Printer
	Calculator	TV Monitor

Our Brain

Our Senses	Our Separate Brain Functions	Our Communication Systems
Hearing	Memory	Talking
Smelling	Language Processing	Writing
Position	Imagination	Gesturing
Vibration	Counting	Drawing
Taste	Music	Facial Looks
Temperature	Calculating	
Vision		

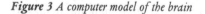

Figure 3 A computer model of the brain

puter speak") represents our memory, judgment, language, counting, facial recognition (crucial in autism), emotional control, self-awareness, the need and ability to relate to others, and all our other intellectual (cognitive) functions. The output part represents talking, writing, drawing, gesturing, kicking the dog, and all the other ways we use to let others know what is going on in our hearts and minds.

With this model in mind, let's start out down the research trail. Our first big goal in the 1960s was to "prove" which one of these two theories was true:

1. autism is caused by "bad psychological parenting" in children with normal brain development (it is a psychological disorder), or

2.   autism is caused by abnormal brain development (it is a
     neurological disorder and psychological factors have nothing to do
     with it).

Of course, our initial feeling was that number two would turn out to be correct, despite the fact that we had been taught in medical school that number
one was correct, and was the prevailing opinion at the time.

Studying brain wave activity

Looking for abnormal brain waves

Early reports in the 1960s suggested that many children who had "autistic
disturbances of affective contact" also had epileptic seizures. In fact, it was
believed at that time that about one third of children with autism also had
epilepsy (called a "seizure disorder"). If this were true it would be a major
clue that brain damage was the cause of autism. This seemed a likely place
to start our search.

    Please allow me a few words of explanation about this type of research
for readers who are not electrophysiologists. Every part of the body puts
out electrical energy (waves). We can easily measure those from the brain,
obviously called "brain waves," by pasting wires on the scalp and connect-
ing them to a recording device called an EEG (electroencephalogram). We
say a person has epilepsy when once in a while they have a seizure and lose
consciousness. Often, though not always, an EEG recording can detect
abnormal waves between actual seizures, when the person appears quite
normal. If we do find such abnormal waves we can give them medicines to
prevent seizures from starting.

    Now let's get back to the research trail. As I said, looking for abnormal
EEG waves in our autistic kids seemed a logical place to start our quest. But
there was a slight problem we had to figure out first. You see, neither my
research colleague, Dr. Edward Ornitz, nor I had been trained in EEG
analysis. We put our heads together and decided to take a short trip. We
went up one whole flight of stairs to the office of Dr. Richard Walter, then
Chief of Neurology. We explained our problem, namely that we had many
ideas and many autistic patients, but needed his help to study them with the
EEG. He lit up with enthusiasm. He too had been perplexed by autism, and
right then and there we made the first of many scientific marriages. We had
the patients; Dr. Walter had a special laboratory. Our academic nuptials
were performed.

But like all marriages, there were difficulties and adjustments to be made. Dr. Walter let us use the EEG laboratory free of charge, but we needed more expert help. Dr. John Hanley, a dear friend and fellow psychiatrist who had special expertise in EEG analysis, volunteered to help us. Mr. Everett Carr and Mrs. Anne Mason Brothers, both research associates, also volunteered their time to help run the equipment and analyze the recordings. All three soon became key members of our research team, and they published many scientific articles on autism with Dr. Ornitz and myself over the next few years.

Our first study involved reading the EEG records on all the autistic children we could find on a "blind basis." That meant that Dr. Hanley and Dr. Walter didn't know if the records they were reading were from autistic kids, or age- and sex-matched kids with other problems, or kids with no problems at all.

For better or worse, after reading the records of over a hundred autistic children we did not find any type of brain wave abnormality that was unique to autism. But to our surprise, only a small percentage of autistic kids had abnormal waves in their EEG recordings at all.

With these results we were able to lay a ghost from the past to rest. Autism and epilepsy are not directly associated. Many other researchers throughout the world have since found the same thing.

Unfortunately, over the past years many kids and adults with autism and no history of seizures have been given needless EEG tests. Worse still, I have heard of countless numbers who have even been given powerful anti-epileptic medications when their EEG tests were normal and they never had a history of seizures. Today we do not even recommend an EEG test unless there is a history of seizures, and we never give anti-seizure medicine unless there is a history of obvious seizures.

Discovering immature sleep patterns

The decades of the 1950s, 1960s, and the 1970s were exciting times for those of us trying to figure out how the brain works, with new discoveries being reported day after day.

Do you recall that I described in chapter 1 how many major scientific discoveries were made in olden days by men armed only with their powers of observation and insatiable curiosity? I referred to them as "seekers," not just "lookers". Well, history tends to repeat itself. And as recently as 1953, a young medical student, following in their footsteps, opened up a whole new field of research. And this new field helped us find evidence of delayed brain development in autism.

Here is what happened in that year. This medical student, Eugene Aserinsky, was asked by his professor, Dr. Nathaniel Kleitman, to watch some infants while they slept and to carefully note everything he saw. He followed his professor's instructions (a remarkable feat for a medical student in and of itself) and did what millions of parents have done since we became humans. He just looked at the sleeping infants. But he did more than just look; he was also seeking to find out what was going on. What he found that was new, what had never been seen before, was that their eyes moved back and forth in rapid bursts beneath their closed lids most of the time they slept. He showed his notes to Dr. Kleitman and their curiosity took off. They wondered what caused these rapid eye movements – did they have a purpose, what did they represent?

Does Dr. Aserinsky's observing rapid eye movements and his wondering with Dr. Kleitman remind you of how Sir Isaac Newton observed an apple falling, and wondered why it fell down and not up? Well it reminds me. And just as Newton discovered gravity by wondering about what he saw, these two doctors discovered that our brain changes the way it works as we sleep. They soon identified several stages of sleep, and called the first one they had noted "rapid eye movement sleep" (soon shortened to REM sleep).

We now know all mammals spend part of their time sleeping in this stage. It is characterized by very fast brain wave activity similar to when we are awake, but nerve filters at the base of the brain prevent us from moving and keep us asleep. These filters turn on and off rapidly producing rapid eye movements, jerky arm and leg movements, rapid heartbeats, and vivid mental images we remember when we wake up as action dreams.

Dr. Ed Ornitz and I were especially intrigued by early reports that the amount of time spent in REM sleep gets shorter and shorter as you get older. While infants spend almost all of their time asleep in the REM stage, we adults spend only about 20 percent of our nights in this stage.

We realized right away that this represents a normal developmental change in the brain. What if there was no such change in autistic kids as they got older? Could this be the "proof" of delayed brain development that we had guessed (hypothesized) occurred in autism? Could we measure it?

We rushed upstairs again and asked Dr. Walter this question. There was good news. His lab was already studying all-night sleep patterns, or "sleep architecture," in adults and we were welcome to record our autistic kids on their "off" nights.

The bad news was that it took so many long hours to obtain and analyze information on each autistic child. Since all-night recordings were needed we had to get each child comfortable enough to sleep through the night in the laboratory with wires glued to their heads. This averaged three nights for each child. Then we had to stay up all night watching over them while they slept, and then face the next day working half asleep ourselves. Finally, in those days, each all-night recording took a week to analyze. These days I can do all the analysis in seconds on my desktop computer.

But the biggest hurdle was the fact that we did not know exactly how brain wave patterns (architecture) changed with age in non-autistic children. To learn this we had to spend countless nights and countless hours getting information on non-autistic age- and sex-matched kids to compare with the autistics.

As luck would have it, many of our research team had little children whom we lured into our sleep lab to be our comparison cases. We did this by offering them the chance to become "Junior Astronauts" who were lucky enough to "fly all night" in our "space station" at the hospital. (Mommy could go along if they wanted her too.) Fortunately, all the kids, both the autistics and non-autistics, fell asleep on time except for one little girl. She was one of my daughters, and she fell soundly asleep only after we gave up at midnight and put her in the car for a ride home. Could that have anything to do with the fact that when she grew up she chose a career putting people to sleep? (She is an anesthesiologist.)

But in spite of all these difficulties our efforts paid off. We discovered that the all-night sleep patterns seen on the EEG were subtly different in the autistics when compared to the non-autistics. While all the stages of sleep were there, they definitely matured more slowly in the autistics. This was the first real measurable evidence ("proof") of delayed brain development in autism.

I want to make it clear that not every autistic child showed the delayed, immature pattern. It only became apparent when we compared groups of age- and sex-matched autistic and non-autistic kids.

Learning that we needed to compare large groups of age- and sex-matched autistic and non-autistic children to find significant differences proved prophetic. It turns out this was something we had to do in all our future studies. Unfortunately, to this day no single test has yet been found that separates all autistics from all non-autistics.

Discovering developmental delays in responses to sounds during sleep

While the kids were sleeping in the EEG lab we also measured how their brain waves responded to sound. We did this by playing soft "clicks" into their room through a little loudspeaker on the wall by their beds. We then measured the response in their brain waves to the clicks.

What we discovered with the "clicks" was most interesting. It was similar to what we had found out about the delayed development of their sleep stages. The brain waves produced by the clicks in autistic children, as a group, failed to mature on schedule. They maintained an infantile pattern much too long.

Finding evidence that sleep patterns (architecture) and responses to sound remain immature confirmed our basic idea of what causes the symptoms of autism. Certainly the frequent reports of unusual sleep cycles and unusual responses to sound sensations (appearing deaf and overreacting to sounds) could be explained this way. Our search for "proof" was beginning to pay off. But let's keep moving down the research trail.

Spinning chairs, movie cameras, and microscopes

Discovering developmental delays in the balance system

After the EEG results were in we looked for a new path to explore. During our observational studies we were struck by how many autistic kids spent hours spinning, twirling, and swinging without getting dizzy. This caught our attention as it could indicate a problem in the part of the brain that adjusts the sensitivity to vestibular (inner ear) stimulation. Perhaps, if we were lucky enough, we could find a way to test this idea with an experiment that wouldn't wind up leaving us sleepy and cranky all day.

As I pondered this problem a memory popped into my mind. It was in the compartment labeled "useless information I had to memorize in medical school, and would probably never use again." What I recalled was that you tested the vestibular system by spinning a patient around in a special swivel chair with a ring around it. After a set number of spins you stopped the chair suddenly by grabbing the ring. Then you timed how long the subject's eyes moved rapidly back and forth with a stopwatch. This gives an objective measure of dizziness. These eye movements after spinning stops are called "post-rotatory nystagmus."

Remembering all this made me smile. I realized it was going to be much easier to test the vestibular system than it had been to say up all night studying brain waves.

A search of the basement at the UCLA medical center turned up a rusted old testing chair. We brought it up to a conference room and scrubbed and greased it till it spun like new. Although the old chair had a ring around it we didn't trust our autistic kids to sit in it alone, so we modified the experiment by having them sit on their (non-autistic) parents' laps. After spinning them to the right, we stopped the chair quickly and timed their dizzy response. Then we did the same thing to the left. Finally, we repeated all the spins in the dark while we measured the duration of their eye movements electronically.

To our surprise, we noted right off the bat that we had a lot of dizzy parents, but the autistic kids were calm as contented clams as soon as the chair stopped. Our stopwatch proved that autistic kids had significantly decreased responses to spinning when the lights were on. However, even more surprising, in the dark both groups had longer responses but there was no longer any difference between them.

This is how the muse of research seduces you. You pose an interesting question, you get an answer, and then that answer poses a host of even more intriguing new questions. We had found one answer; yes there was a difference between the autistics and the non-autistics, but only when we tested them in the light, and not in the dark.

How to explain this unexpected and perplexing discovery? We were able to ascertain that the difference in responses was not age related. My best guess was, and still is, the part of the brain that coordinates the two different sensations, vision and spinning, is not fully developed in the autistic kids. But in the dark, with only one sensation to handle, spinning, the brain of the autistic child functions just as well as the non-autistic brain.

Here was subtle but definite evidence of brain dysfunction in the systems that turn up and turn down the volume, or adjust our sensitivity to sensations. Recall the term I told you Dr. Ed Ornitz coined to describe our observation of how autistic kids go from over- to underreacting to sensations? It was "perceptual inconstancy." Well, the results of our vestibular experiments certainly point a way to understanding how the brain can dampen a response when two sensory sensations come in together, and yet respond normally when one comes in alone.

Discovering a "release mechanism" like Parkinson's disease in autism

We designed a third early study to test our idea that the rhythmic hand flapping seen so often in autistic kids was due to brain dysfunction, and was not just an emotional release, which was the accepted view at the time. It was generally thought at that time to be simply an expression of emotional distress, a form of learned behavior that could be "unlearned" by conditioning.

We figured that if repetitive hand flapping was voluntary and due to emotional distress the speed of the flapping would change as the child became more or less emotional (frustrated, angry, or whatever), and that different kids would flap at different speeds. On the other hand (pardon the pun), if it was driven by abnormal brain function, then all autistic kids should flap at about the same speed. Also, once they start they shouldn't speed up and slow down. They should start at cruising speed, and stay there till they stopped. This is the case with hand tremors in Parkinson's disease. In this neurological disease all patients flap at about the same speed, and start and maintain that speed till they stop.

To test this idea I "liberated" an old silent 16 millimeter movie camera from my father's office, one he had gotten years before as a gift from the Kodak Company for helping them develop X-ray film. Then, with their parents' permission of course, we took movies of a large number of autistic kids who were "frequent hand flappers." Finally we played the movies back at slow speed and counted the number of flaps per minute.

We discovered, to our delight, that our idea was correct. All the kids we filmed at UCLA flapped at about the same speed, and started and kept it steady till they stopped. We put icing on the cake by taking similar high-speed movies of many autistic kids in other cities around the country. Wherever they came from, they flapped at the same speed, and maintained the same speed while they were flapping. There was no relationship between how the kids felt (happy, sad, angry) and the speed of their flapping.

These results helped us debunk the theory that flapping was emotionally driven, caused by psychological poisoning from bad parents, or just learned. They provide another step on the road to "proving" that abnormal brain development was the culprit causing autism.

Discovering differences in brain structure

Many diseases have yielded their secrets to pathologists, the physicians who perform autopsies. I spent several horrible half summers earning money to finance my mountaineering trips while in college by working in the autopsy room at the Boston City Hospital. It was my duty to clean the autopsy tables, swab the floors, and put specimens in formaldehyde for the doctors to examine. Formaldehyde has an irritating repulsive smell that sticks to your skin and clothes no matter how hard and how often you try to scrub it off. I lost all my friends while working there. If you have never smelled formaldehyde, take my advice, don't.

But to return to our research, this experience taught me the value of pathological studies, a lesson I was eager to apply help solve the mystery of autism. At the time we began our work there was no firm autopsy (neuropathological) information on autism in the medical literature. With this in mind, I designed the first prospective autopsy study of autism in 1976. It was the most emotionally painful project I have ever undertaken. Every time I gave a talk to a parent or professional group I would interrupt myself somewhere and say:

> I have to interrupt this talk for a sad "commercial." I know it is a hard subject to think about, but if you know of a person with autism who dies suddenly from an accident, or after an illness, please have the family contact me at UCLA at once as we are conducting an autopsy research project.

I would then go on to briefly describe our research goals and beg for cooperation. As I was giving lectures to parent groups in almost every state and province in Canada to help them get started or to grow, the word spread. Over the next six years we were contacted by a dozen families who had lost an autistic child to illness or an accident, and obtained autopsy materials from four of them.

Needing help to study the autopsy specimens when they started arriving, I took another trip upstairs. This time it was a long one, all of three flights of stairs to get to the office of Dr. Arnold Schibel. He was then the director of the Brain Research Institute at UCLA and a world famous neuropathologist. He too was intrigued and readily volunteered his time and his laboratory facilities. One of his graduate students, Taihung Duong, also volunteered to join our research team.

It took several years before we had collected enough research materials to begin analyzing them under the microscope. What we found was that from the outside the brains looked normal enough. But on looking through the microscope we saw a significant decrease in the number of a special type of cell in the part of the brain called the cerebellum. These cells were simply missing. They had failed to develop. These special cells are called "Purkinji cells," named after the famous Czechoslovakian pathologist who first described them. Purkinji cells are very large and are usually arranged in a neat row, like chairs around a table. In the autistics it looked like every second or third chair was missing.

Fortunately for the field of autism, just about that time two young doctors from Boston became just as interested in studying the structure of the brain as we were. They had heard of our autopsy project and called. We were delighted that they wanted to expand the research in this area and we arranged to meet in Los Angeles. Over a pizza lunch at Mario's, our favorite spot in the West Wood Village (don't bother to look for it, it has morphed into a California Pizza Kitchen) we proposed yet another professional marriage. However, it was only after Dr. Margaret Bauman and Dr. Jack Kemper agreed that LA pizza was just as good as Boston pizza that we consummated this new research marriage.

Because they had more sophisticated equipment, and because this was to become the main focus of their research efforts, and because we were busy with other projects at the time, we shipped all our research materials to them in order to help jump-start their work. They more than fulfilled the promises they made that day over pepperoni and mushrooms. They have continued to make significant contributions to our knowledge of autism to this day. We all owe them a debt of gratitude for their pioneering work and for having stayed focused on helping unravel the mysteries of autism.

Dr. Bauman, Dr. Kemper, and others who followed have demonstrated subtle anatomical differences in the brain structure of some patients with "primary" (no cause known) autism. No specific "smoking gun" has turned up yet, but the hunt is still on in pathology laboratories all over the world today as I write.

Neurotransmitters and "Nervous Mice"
Discovering abnormal levels of chemical messengers in the brain

When I was in medical school the current wisdom was that the brain was wired like an old-fashioned telephone switchboard or computer chip. An electrical signal was thought to travel down a nerve until it got to the end, where it "sparked" or jumped over to travel down to the end of the next nerve, jump over, and so on.

That was a great theory, but it turned out to be all wrong. In the 1950s and 1960s we discovered that nature had evolved a much more complex system than we ever imagined. It turns out that the way a nerve signal travels from one nerve cell to the next one down the line is not electrical at all, but chemical. Now we know that when a nerve signal gets to the end of one nerve special chemicals, called neurotransmitters, are released into the space between it and the next nerve down the line. This space, called a synapse, is very small, and the neurotransmitter quickly crosses the gap. When it arrives at the next nerve cell it starts a signal there. This chemical then gets taken back up by the first nerve it left from, and waits to take another trip across the synapse when the next signal comes down the line. This process of being taken back is called "re-uptake."

This may seem complicated, but nature designed it, not some crazy scientist who was trying to get you to flunk high school biology. Please try to picture in your mind this "put it out" — "take it back up" cycle of chemical messengers going on between nerve cells. This is how one nerve cell "talks" to the next one down the line and keeps the signal going. Keeping this picture in mind will help you understand our subsequent experiments with medicines to treat autism.

Two of the first psychiatrists to study these chemical messengers happened to be on the faculty of UCLA Medical School when Dr. Ed Ornitz and I were concluding our all-night brain wave studies. They were our friends Dr. Rick Schain and Dr. Danny Freedman. The minute I found out what they were up to I thought, "Could weird abnormal chemical messages in the brain cause autism?" Looking back now I realize that this was not exactly the way to state a scientific hypothesis; I never would use those words on a grant application, but facts are facts.

The trip to their lab was only down one flight of stairs. They gave me the best advice I could have asked for when they said:

> Sorry, we are working on something else now, but here's what you need to do. Hop in that old excuse for a car you drive and go across Wilshire Boulevard to the Brentwood Veterans Administration Hospital Neurobiochemistry Laboratory. Look up these two guys, Art Yuweiler and Ed Geller. They run the lab and know more about this business of neurotransmitters than anyone east of the Pacific Ocean.

I got in my old car, which chose to start that day with no trouble, a good sign to begin with, and drove over to the VA looking for a big shiny building. Instead I found a doublewide trailer that housed the laboratory of these two world-class neurobiochemists. Only their names in tiny letters at the bottom of the door let me know where they worked. I am proud to say that we became fast friends as well as colleagues, and remain so to this day with Art Yuweiler. Unfortunately, Ed Geller passed away a few years ago. I am proud to honor his memory and his contributions to autistic research. And the icing on this cake is that all the contributions these two made were done on their own time, nights and weekends, and on a voluntary basis.

Art and Ed suggested that the neurotransmitter called serotonin (5-hydroxy-trypamine) was most likely the villain we were looking for.

They guessed this because in studies of rats, where it had been found in the brain stem, it was evident that it was involved somehow with sleep cycles. But they had some bad news. They told me it would be impossible to test serotonin in our patients because the test method was time-consuming and crude, to say the least.

It seems the way you tested serotonin in those days started out in a fish store where you bought a bunch of clams. No, I am not fooling. You opened a live clam, tied a tiny string to his (or her, we were never sure) heart, and hooked it up to a device which recorded the clam's pulse rate. Then onto the heart you squirted a solution with a known amount of serotonin in it and took the pulse. Next you squirted in the solution with an unknown amount of serotonin from the patient, and checked the pulse again. The difference between the pulse rates let you figure out how much serotonin was in the patient's sample.

Being a clam chowder lover (remember I told you I was raised in New England), I insisted we develop a new type of test for serotonin that would spare the lives of my favorite chowder ingredient. But seriously, we needed a rapid and accurate test for serotonin, and that was the first step we had to take. It took over a year to accomplish, but it resulted in a test that became the worldwide standard test for serotonin.

The next big problem we had to figure out was pretty obvious – we wanted to know what was going on with serotonin in the brain. But how could we do this without taking out a piece of the brain, an obvious impossibility?

Fortunately there were a few reports in the scientific literature that serotonin is carried in the blood by cells called platelets. Best of all for us was the fact that they carry serotonin just like brain cells do. Also, human and animal studies comparing blood and brain serotonin levels had shown a close relationship between the two. When one was up so was the other, and when one was below normal so was the other. Armed with this information and our new test, we were on our way.

Over the next few years we measured serotonin blood levels and platelet counts in literally hundreds of autistic and non-autistic infants, children, and adults. I crossed the United States, Europe, and South America, a medical vampire armed with syringes and needles.

Needless to say, I had a few wild adventures along the way. For example, I was in Paris getting a blood sample from an autistic girl who had an autistic sister, and needed to get a sample from her non-autistic brother for our family studies. He was willing, but there was a little geographical problem. He lived in New Zealand and was on his way to Toronto via London while I was in Paris seeing his sister.

A light bulb flashed in my head when he told me he had a brief layover at Heathrow Airport in London. I hopped across the channel, as they say over there. We met, and went to a men's room so I could wash up before drawing his blood sample. I was "scrubbing up," he rolled up his sleeve, and then – bang! we stopped cold. It dawned on us at the same instant that we would both wind up in jail if an airport policeman walked in and caught me sticking a needle in his arm. Then another light bulb went on in the brother's head, and he suggested we find the airport first aid office. There we explained the experiment to a bemused nurse, who finally agreed to let us continue with our experiment.

I am often asked if a lot of kids fainted when I drew their blood. I am proud, or should I say lucky, to have had only one fainting episode. It happened in a small living room in a small house in St. Louis. I was busy doing my "needle in the arm" thing with a little girl whose father was holding her on his lap. She was smiling and telling me about her brand new puppy when, with no warning, we heard a loud CLUNK from across the room. You guessed it. Her mother had fainted, fallen off a couch, and was stretched out on the rug. We rushed over, but by the time we got to her she was up and suffered only some wounded pride.

We measured many other things besides just serotonin blood levels. We also checked levels around the clock to determine if there were circadian rhythm differences. We studied family patterns and looked for correlations with IQ, severity of symptoms, multiple family incidences of autism, age, sex, and as many other factors as we could think up. In short, we measured all the measurements we could think to measure.

And now, you want to know what we discovered? The simple answer is we discovered another developmental delay!

Our non-autistic comparison subjects started off in infancy with high levels of serotonin that gradually decreased until their teen years. In most, but not all, of our autistic patients, serotonin levels started high in infancy and stayed high as they grew older!

No, unfortunately we had not found a "smoking gun." Some autistics had serotonin levels in the normal range. Also, serotonin levels did not correlate with any of the other factors we looked at (IQ, sex, early or late onset of symptoms, the presence of autistic siblings in the family, race, where they were from, etc.).

Many other scientists around the world have also studied serotonin levels. We collaborated on two such studies. One was in France with Dr. Gloria

Laxer, the mother of an autistic boy with whom I co-authored a book about autism, and the other was in England with Sir Michael Rutter. The results of these studies were similar to what we found at our VA laboratory in Los Angeles. The common denominator was evidence of delayed development of a biological system, in this case, the neurotransmitter serotonin.

Discovering an abnormal reflex in the eye

I came upon, or I should say I stumbled upon, our next stop along the research trail in a very strange manner. And it led to a strange land where I learned much about how our eyes change light waves into nerve impulses. Also, I learned a lot about a hormone called melatonin, the one we put out into our bloodstream when we sleep. These were things that I had not been taught about when I was in medical school only a few years before because they had not yet been discovered. The miracles of modern medical science are truly wondrous to behold.

Here's how it happened. A local hospital had invited me to give a lecture on autism, and the audience was the usual group of gray-haired middle-aged physicians. What caught my eye as I started talking was a young man in the front row. He looked familiar. Was he one of my medical students? Yes he was. How flattered I felt, but only for a moment. A closer look and I realized that indeed he was one of my medical students, but the one who had a serious crush on one of his classmates, who just happened to be, by a remote chance, one of my daughters. "What a cool way to impress the 'old man,'" I thought as I launched into my lecture.

Soon I got to the point of describing how autistic children often flap their hands and lamented that we did not have an animal with similar behavior to study. At this point, Rob —, the medical student whose identity I will guard with my life, raised his hand. (By the way, his love was unrequited, my daughter eventually married another medical student and is now a psychiatrist herself.)

"Dr. Ritvo, what about that well-known genetic strain of mice, the ones called 'Nervous Mice'? They rhythmically shake their paws for hours. Could they be like autistic kids?" Rob asked.

"Of course, that's a very interesting question," I said in my most professorial tone. "I would love to discuss it with you when we have more time. Why don't you come to my office at school next week and we'll talk about it?"

Only now, years later, can I confess that my "of course" did not mean: "Of course I know all about what you are talking about." No, it meant: "I don't have a ghost of an idea what you're talking about, I need some time to go to the library and find out what the devil these little mice are all about." Nervous Mice were as foreign to me as three-legged dogs or nervous pigs.

What I found out in the library was astounding. Yes, there was a strain of mice that did flap their paws rhythmically. And yes, there was even a professor at Harvard Medical School who had devoted years of research to understanding what was wrong with their nervous system.

By the time Rob arrived at my office I had our research team up to speed. We spent many exciting hours brainstorming possible connections between what had been found in these mice and what we could study in our autistic patients. First, it had been found that they had abnormal sperm cells. This proved a dead end because we couldn't figure out a way to get sperm samples from our autistic boys without facing serious jail time.

So we turned to another abnormal thing that had been found in these poor mice, an abnormal reflex in their eyes. Specifically, these mice had a decreased electrical response to flashing lights on a test called the electroretinogram (ERG) test. Of course, at this point I could hardly remember what that test was. However, we got quite excited because it looked like we could test this reflex in our kids' eyes safely and without any risk of going to jail.

Then I suddenly remembered that a member of our Utah research team, Mrs. Carmen Pingree, had a friend in the Department of Ophthalmology at the University of Utah. I immediately called her. She immediately called her friend who immediately called me back. When I asked if we could test similar responses in the eyes of autistic children he said, "Of course." (By now I hated those words.) "All you have to do is give them the ERG test, you know what that is, don't you?"

"Of course," I said, knowing a trip to the library was just around the corner.

To make a long story short, we traveled to Utah where were already conducting research in collaboration with doctors at the University of Utah on genetics. Mr. Donald Creel of the ophthalmology department showed us a teaching film he had made that explained the ERG test. He volunteered to join our research team and donated countless hours to the cause of understanding autism. He tested dozens of autistic and age- and sex-matched non-autistic kids and adults for us – at no charge.

In order to broaden our sample of patients we arranged for ERG testing in Los Angeles, Boston, and Washington, DC. But there was a slight problem. In order to standardize the tests we needed to have some of the same people tested at each location. Carmen came through in grand style, agreeing to fly around the country with her autistic son Brian. We eventually crowned them "The Transcontinental Queen and The Prince of ERG Testing."

After standardizing the test this way we were able to compare over a dozen autistic kids, their parents, and some of their siblings and grandparents who lived in different cities.

What we discovered was quite surprising. Some, but not all, of the autistic kids had abnormally decreased responses to light flashes as measured on their ERG tests. All other tests of their vision and their optic nerves we conducted were normal.

In an independent study, our friend and colleague Dr. George Realmuto confirmed our results. His research team at the University of Minnesota obtained abnormal ERG recordings from most of his sample of autistic children.

Now the beauty and frustration of research again struck us. The beauty is in the new finding, the frustration is in the new mystery of the "Why?" the finding creates.

I spent many dull hours reading and ruminating about what could cause the decreased ERG response. I learned that the electrical response we were measuring came from special cells in the retina that used a chemical messenger called dopamine. Could there be too little dopamine being made in these retinal cells, or could there be something blocking it from working? There was nothing in the library I could find of help, so I took to boring my friends and colleagues by asking them, and everyone else I met who might know.

Persistence paid off. During a research meeting on genetics in Boston I met a young graduate student who was studying nerve signals in the brains of a species of transparent fish. (Yes, there are transparent fish, and yes, there are scientists who devote their lives to learning how brains send signals from one nerve cell to another by using these fish.) In the middle of our conversation about our favorite baseball team, the Red Sox, I asked him, just offhand, if he had any ideas about what could cause decreased ERG responses in our autistic kids. He gave me a curious look and said in a condescending tone the magic words I hated, but was hoping to hear: "Of course! Don't you know that the hormone melatonin blocks the effects of dopamine?"

This rolled off his tongue like he was talking to the village idiot. By now I was mature enough to say: "Hell no. I don't have a ghost of an idea what you're talking about. Would you let me buy you a cup of coffee? I'm a big spender from out West, and you could explain to me how melatonin blocks dopamine. It may help me figure out why some of my little autistic kids have abnormal eye tests."

He took me up on my generous offer of free coffee, he explained all he knew about melatonin and dopamine, and it led to another branch of our research trail, this one called "Melatonin Land."

I couldn't wait till I got back to Los Angeles so I called Art Yuweiler at the VA Neurobiochemistry Lab long distance. When I told him I was flying back on the "red eye" and couldn't wait to start off on a new tangent, he told me to "calm down and think good thoughts" (a philosophy he liked to practice). He promised to clear the decks for a meeting as soon as I hit town.

True to his word, next morning he was waiting for Riva and me with his colleagues, Dr. Bremer, Dr. Raleigh, and Selma Plotkin to hear the news.

As luck would have it they were quite familiar with melatonin. It is a hormone that is made by a tiny pea-shaped gland located at the base of the brain, called the pineal gland. This gland is connected by special nerves to the eyes. When it gets dark at night it starts to make melatonin, which it pours into the bloodstream. The amount of melatonin in the blood reaches its peak about two in the morning, and then the pineal gland shuts down, the melatonin level rapidly drops, and it is all gone by sunrise.

There was good news and bad news, as always. The good news was that the VA lab was set up to measure melatonin and they would do it free of charge. The bad news was that we were back in the "vampire business" of drawing blood samples from kids and their parents again.

After many months of work we discovered that some, though not all, of the autistic children and adults we tested had measurable amounts of melatonin in their blood during the day. This explained the decreased ERG responses we had found. Namely, daytime melatonin was blocking the dopamine needed to make a normal ERG response in the eyes of some of the autistic kids.

But more to the point, we had discovered another developmental delay, this time in the endocrine or gland system. Most likely, this means that there is also abnormal regulation of dopamine in the brain, not just in the eyes. It appears that both serotonin and dopamine fail to develop adult patterns in autism. Instead of starting high in infancy and then dropping gradually to lower levels by adulthood, in autism they both start high and stay high.

Some concluding comments

I apologize if some of the research experiments I have just described were hard to follow. But nature designed our bodies in a very complicated and mysterious way, and there is just no way to simplify it to remove the mysteries.

But let's return to the big research questions we set out to answer at the beginning of this chapter. The answer, or "the bottom line" as my business friends like to say, is this: autism and Asperger's disorder are caused by abnormal development of the brain, not by psychological factors like bad parenting or emotional traumas. They are "neurological" not "psychological" disorders. We have found solid evidence that some of the parts develop slowly and at irregular rates. They either don't "come online" at all, or do so later than normally expected. This causes the persistence of infantile patterns of sensory-motor responses, language development, and the capacity to relate to others and objects. Their failure to mature on schedule causes all the symptoms that plague those with autism and Asperger's disorder.

Chapter 5

Searching
for Causes

Now that you understand the nature of the symptoms and the developmental delays in the brain that produce them, it is time to follow our medical model of disease and look for a cause or causes.

Before tackling this question I want to remind you that we are dealing with a syndrome. As I explained before, syndromes are diseases that are defined by the problems they lead to, and usually have many different causes. For instance, hypertension (high blood pressure), pneumonia, arthritis, and heart attacks are all common syndromes, and each obviously has many different causes.

When we do not know the cause of a syndrome we call it a "primary syndrome." When and if we are lucky enough to find a cause in a particular patient we still keep the label syndrome, but say it is "secondary" or caused by this factor. For instance, if a patient with pneumonia is found to have tuberculosis, we say his pneumonia is "secondary" to TB. This all may seem a bit confusing right now, but it is important because we shall soon be talking about "primary" and "secondary" autism.

Searching medical histories for possible causes

Our quest for the cause (or causes) began as soon as we started our research program in the 1960s. For a start, Dr. Ornitz and our team put together a 500-item questionnaire for all our parents to fill out. They quickly dubbed it "War and Peace" since it took so long to read and complete. It asked about every factor we could think of that might even remotely be at fault.

After analyzing the results of hundreds of questionnaires we came up empty-handed. Let me stress that there were no pregnancy, delivery, medical, diet, vaccination, food or other allergy problems, infections, medical treatments, nor a host of other factors we asked about, that were different between the autistic patients and their non-autistic siblings or the general population.

Only two exceptions in the lives of the autistics singled out possible causative factors. The first was if an autistic child had another disease that was known to cause brain damage and developmental delays that mimicked the symptoms of autism. These cases we classified as having secondary autism.

The best example of secondary autism is the one caused by German measles. It's called "post-rubella autism." In a small percentage of children with rubella the virus attacks the brain. Depending on the age of the child and the part of the brain infected, a child can show symptoms that are seen in autism for a year or two. Then they disappear. Only while these symptoms are present do we say the child has "secondary autism," or "rubella autism." Fortunately, this type of secondary autism is very rare.

The second exception that distinguished certain autistic children was the presence of a parent or sibling who also had autism. These children we said have "familial autism," and I shall discuss them in great detail in a later section of this chapter.

Our "Rolls Royce" study in Utah

Since our questionnaire had not uncovered a cause for the vast majority of cases, and since we hadn't yet won the Nobel Prize, we needed to look deeper. We put our heads together, did some brainstorming, and dreamed up a "Rolls Royce" research project. It was to be loaded with all the "bells and whistles" we could think of.

We knew we would need to survey a large stable population of over one or two million people, not just those who came to UCLA for care. We needed a place where we could contact every hospital, clinic, school, pediatrician, and social service agency. We needed a place where most of the people were medically sophisticated, concerned for their children, and would be willing to participate in our research. And most important, we needed a place where the "gene pool" represented that of the entire United States and Europe.

As I was thinking about all these requirements a name suddenly popped into my tired mind, Mrs. Carmen Pingree. Carmen and her husband John had recently come from Salt Lake City to consult me about their autistic son, Brian, and we had become friends. As chairman of the Professional Advisory Panel of the Autism Society of America I knew of her efforts to establish a chapter in Utah and to open a special education school for autistic kids in Salt Lake City.

A quick detour for a peek at "parent power"

To digress for a moment, I want to share with you the fascinating story of how Carmen got the first special education classes for autistic children in Utah started. She began by making a home movie about autism and bought a portable tabletop projector. Then she got on the phone and made appointments with each and every state legislator. Then she dragged her "dog and pony" show to their offices, and sat with them to make sure they watched her film. Then she had a bill introduced into the state legislature authorizing special education for autistic children. And then, *voilà!* an old closed-down school was reopened and the first special education classes for autistic children appeared in Utah.

While on the subject of "parent power," there is another heartwarming wonderful example I want to share with you. This one took place in North Carolina. Parents there were confronted with the same problem. There were no services for autistic children in the state, and pleas to their lawmakers had fallen on deaf ears. They got together and realized that since "The Lord helps those who help themselves," they had to take matters into their own hands. A plan was devised. They invited each state legislator to a Sunday brunch for an innocuous purpose related to helping sick children. When the legislators arrived at the hotel they were escorted to a banquet hall where they found one large round table in the middle of the room. Chairs encircled the table and every other chair had a place card with the name of a legislator on it. Once they were seated, in came a group of severely autistic kids whose parents placed them in the seats between the startled legislators. Needless to say, the kids were not chosen because they had good table manners. Their parents took seats around the edge of the room and watched in horror and delight as their government got a firsthand lesson on how to dine with a severely autistic child (flying food and all).

The dinner yielded a fabulous dessert. Funds were quickly voted to establish a network of clinics around the state devoted to the diagnosis and treatment of autism. Two young men were hired to run the clinics, and they subsequently devoted their careers to autism research. Dr. Eric Schopler and Robert Reichler established programs that serve even today as models for the rest of the world. Among their many contributions was the development of a special education program called the TEACCH method (Teaching and Education of Autistic and related Communication handicapped CHildren). Oh yes, the dessert also had whipped cream on top. That was a small private plane that they were given to visit their autism clinics throughout the state.

Utah becomes "The Place"

Let's return to our research trail.

When I put all the requirements for our "Rolls Royce" research project down on paper, and thought of Utah and Carmen, the words of a famous Mormon pioneer, Brigham Young, popped into my mind. When he first saw the Great Salt Lake he said, "This is The Place." I paraphrased his words and said to myself, "Could this be the place?" I then answered myself, "Of course it could be the place, let's find out."

A call to Utah resulted in more than I could have hoped for. Carmen invited our entire research team to Salt Lake City. She arranged meetings with doctors from the University of Utah who she knew had an interest in autism. In a few short weeks we formed the UCLA–University of Utah Autism Research Project. Doctors Bill Jensen, Bill McMahon, P. Brent Peterson, and L.B. Jorde volunteered their time and expertise. Research headquarters were set up in Carmen's living room, funding was supplied by a grant from the National Institute of Mental Health, and we were off and running.

Utah proved to be an ideal place to conduct our type of "epidemiological" research. Eighty percent of the people lived along a valley corridor about 100 miles long and 50 miles across at its widest point. This meant most everyone would be easy to reach with a short drive. Also, folks there tended to have large families and did not move around much, providing a stable population base. About 70 percent of all the people in Utah at that time belonged to the Church of Jesus Christ of the Latter Day Saints, commonly called the Mormon Church. This was particularly good news for our research for three reasons.

First, the vast majority of Mormons in Utah were converts from all over the country and Europe. This meant that Utah's gene pool was typical of the entire United States and Europe. This fact had been proven years before by the National Institute of Health which funds genetic research in Utah on many diseases such as high blood pressure and heart disease.

Second, the Mormon Church requires its members to record their family histories for religious purposes. Thus, asking for family information (genealogy) was simply digging in familiar territory for most of those we interviewed.

Third, they tend to have large families, and the more children the better for the type of family studies we wanted to conduct.

Also, luckily for us, there was only one state mental hospital in all of Utah for disabled children and the director was very helpful. In fact, my daughter Anne, who was in college at that time, spent a summer working in this hospital as a member of our research team. And it just happens that this is the very same daughter who, when she was a little girl all those many years before, was the one and only child who wouldn't fall asleep during our all-night sleep studies. Was she paying us back by working there?

Support for our study came from many places. Some were expected, like families in the Autism Society, pediatricians, teachers, caseworkers, and other professionals. Some were unexpected. For instance, two of the leaders of the Mormon Church met with us personally. They and several legislators, clergymen and rabbis volunteered to publicize our case-finding efforts. We got free "spots" on local TV and radio stations, and dozens of newspaper write-ups. Even Senator Oren Hatch asked the public to help us identify any and all developmentally disabled people under the age of 25 in the state. We were very lucky indeed to have found Carmen and the people of Utah.

Over the next year and a half we cast a wide net and identified everyone 25 or younger who could possibly have had autism in the whole state. This part of the research was called the "ascertainment" or "case finding" phase. Our net snared 483 possible cases.

When we felt comfortable that we had found all the potential cases we could, Mrs. Anne Mason Brothers, our research administrator, and her staff took over. They gathered the medical and educational records of each one as well as their parents' answers to Dr. Ornitz's 500-item questionnaire. They then designed a special computer program to store all this information and got it ready for statistical analysis.

The diagnostic phase of the project came next. Here two members of the clinical team conducted independent diagnostic evaluation on each of the 483 possibly autistic cases. (Some were done at the University of Utah, some at the special school for autistic children, some in Carmen's living room, and some in unlikely places like a hamburger stand when that's as close to the clinic as one mother was willing to get.)

Each of the doctors was kept "blind" as to what the other thought until they were finished. Almost all of the time they reached the same diagnosis. When a rare disagreement did occur we held a conference to find out why. It usually turned out that the child's history had been inadequate and both doctors had found it hard to reach a diagnosis (for example, one adopted five-year-old child had no early developmental history). Fortunately this happened so few times that it did not interfere with our statistical analyses.

Evidentially, 241 of the original 483 cases met our research criteria for autism. They provided a goldmine from which we dug many nuggets of new information over the next several years. Here are some of our results.

What we found
The three types of autism

With regard to the $64,000 question – What causes autism? – right off the bat our survey of Utah showed that all the cases fell into one of three groups.

1. *Primary autism*: 80 percent of the cases had no causative factors we could identify.

2. *Secondary autism*: 10 percent of the cases had another disease known to cause brain damage. At the time these patients were seen their clinical picture fitted the diagnostic criteria for autism.

3. *Familial autism*: 10 percent of the cases had a close relative (mother, father, sister, or brother) who also had autism.

We were surprised by four other quite unexpected results that begged for explanation.

Possible causes we looked for but did not find

First, we were surprised and dismayed by the fact that no clear-cut cause emerged right off the bat for 80 percent of the total cases. We reached this conclusion after carefully reviewing all the children's computer-coded re-cords. These included Dr. Ornitz's 500-item questionnaire, their parents' and their medical histories, and their developmental histories.

While we found a wide variety of interesting medical problems, unfor-tunately none proved to be significantly related to autism. On the contrary, the medical histories of all the autistic patients were quite similar to their non-autistic brothers and sisters, and to age- and sex-matched non-autistic comparison children from Utah. This allowed us to discard some of the old and new theories as to what caused autism. For instance, no psychological factors were found in the parents to account for autism. Trauma, neglect, the presence or absence of a mother or father, economic class, educational class, alcohol and drug use, psychosis, divorce, happy marriage, unhappy marriage, parental illnesses, pregnancy history, type of delivery, etc. all proved *not* to be associated with having an autistic child.

Likewise, comparing the autistic children with their non-autistic siblings in the general Utah population failed to show anything special in their medical histories, as had been proposed before by others. The autistic children had the same rate of colds, ear infections, allergies, and all other diseases. They had the same number of vaccinations, immune deficiencies, immune diseases, vitamin deficiencies, celiac or digestive disorders, or food sensitivities. In fact, there was no evidence that they had excess number of diseases of any kind. And there was also no evidence that they had been exposed to toxins such as lead and mercury more than their non-autistic relatives or the general population.

At the present time, 2006, there is renewed interest in the research community in trying to find environmental factors that could cause certain cases of autism. We hope that with new techniques and increased funding this research will pay off, and we will be able to discover previously unde-tectable causes. That is always the hope, not just the goal, of researchers everywhere, and the "light at the end of the tunnel" that guides them.

Brothers and sisters with autism

A second thing that astounded us was the number of families with more than one autistic child. We had been keeping records of twins and families with two or more autistic children at UCLA in a project called "The UCLA Registry for Genetic Studies of Autism" since 1980. By 1985 we had al-ready found a total of 40 pairs of twins in which at least one of the pair had autism. Of these, 23 pairs were identical, and 17 non-identical. In 96 per-cent (22 of 23) of the identical twin pairs both twins were autistic, whereas in only 24 percent (4 of 17) of the non-identical pairs of twins were both autistic.

Also, we had many families with two, three, or four (and one family with five!) autistic siblings. However, we could not figure out how common our multiple-incidence families at UCLA were in the general population. Such information, called the "prevalence" of a disorder, can only be deter-mined if you know the total size of the population from which your cases come. And since UCLA attracted families from literally all over the world we had no way of estimating our population base.

In Utah we eventually identified 17 families with two autistic children, one family with three, one with four, and one with five autistic siblings.

Parents with autism and Asperger's disorder

Our third unexpected discovery was that some parents of our autistic children had previously undiagnosed autism or Asperger's disorder themselves. Here's how I found this out. The scene is the home of an autistic child in our Utah study: "Dr. Ritvo, I want you to take Dad into the living room and talk to him for a bit, I think he is a lot like Johnny, our autistic son." (Said while making a circular motion with a finger at the side of her head, meaning unknown.)

And another time: "Doctor, would you mind looking at my wife, I think she has 'a hair of the dog' that bit our autistic daughter?"

Needless to say, at first I took such requests with a grain of salt. But I always kept an open mind and followed their requests. Before I knew it, we had identified several parents who obviously had autism or Asperger's disorder since childhood, who had grown up, gotten married, and had autistic children.

By the time we completed our work in Utah we had identified 14 such parents. Since they had been found because they had autistic children, we could not draw any conclusions about a specific type of genetic transmission from one generation to the next. Only future surveys of many such parents who are initially found because they have autism or Asperger's disorder, not because their children do, will show what percentage of their children are destined to be affected.

These parents we found were a unique group of people. Each still had symptoms, some obvious, some subtle. Each had married a very devoted caregiving type of person who recognized their "problems in getting along with people," their "strange habits and mannerisms," and their "peculiar interests."

By the way, our scientific report on these autistic parents was the hardest one we ever had getting accepted for publication. We got seven rejection letters before an acceptance finally arrived. None of the reviewers or editors believed us at the time, but today it is a commonly accepted fact that autistic children can grow up to get married and have children.

The relationship between autism and Asperger's disorder

The fourth finding that surprised us was the number of adults who were reported to have had classic symptoms of autism when they were kids, but "outgrew" it and wound up in adulthood as non-diagnosed "odd ducks."

While they were too old to include in our autistic patient population, we gathered as much information on them as we could. These folks, whose symptoms were present but not sufficiently bothersome to require medical attention, we said had "subclinical" autism or Asperger's disorder. The first paper we published describing this type of patient was in 1985. It is entitled "Autism: Forme fruste," which means a partial or very mild type.

At about this time, the late 1980s, while we were busy in Utah, a few clinicians and researchers in the United States and Europe were recognizing the connection between Asperger's and Kanner's work. There were originally two groups of thought. Some, the "splitters," thought autism and Asperger's disorder were two separate and distinct disorders. Others, the "lumpers," thought they were the same disorder, only differing by the degree of severity.

My wife Riva, who had married me at that time only on the condition that she be allowed to join our research team, devoted many hours to studying these subclinical cases.

Riva found many common factors among these mild autistic and Asperger's patients, and no unique or distinguishing features. In all cases we could explain their symptoms as due to developmental delays as we have described before. Based on her research we soon became lumpers. As we indicated in our earlier chapter on the history of these disorders, we "lumpers" have won the test of time. Today, the two are recognized as being mild and severe forms of the same developmental disorder. This is why they are sometimes grouped together and referred to as "pervasive developmental disorders," or "autism spectrum disorders."

Questions of genetics

The recurrence risk estimate

An obvious question that I hear all the time from the parents of my young autistic patients is this: "Doctor Ritvo, what are the chances of us having another autistic child?" or "Dr. Ritvo, do you recommend we stop now or go ahead with our plans to have another child?" (And they usually continue "and don't beat around the bush, what would you do if you were in our shoes?")

Before our Utah study there was no scientific information to guide us in answering these vital questions. However, with the assistance of a colleague from Pennsylvania, Dr. Marshall B. ("Brush") Jones, we were able to conduct a sophisticated statistical analysis of our Utah families and determined what is called the "recurrence risk estimate." This analysis gave us the odds of a family having a second autistic child.

What we found was that the odds are roughly 10 percent (one in ten births) that the next child after an autistic one is born will also have autism. I use the word "roughly" because these statistics are hard to determine. Unlike cards or dice, we don't have many deals or rolls to analyze. Also, after a family has one autistic child they tend to stop having children. While this may be good for them, it limits our ability to figure out the true odds accurately.

This brings up the subject of "genetic counseling." When it comes to answering questions about having more children or not, I simply tell parents the results of our research. I am always very careful not to interject my own opinion. This is a principle that guides all physicians who do genetic counseling. To some parents odds of 10 percent sound very low, and they are encouraged to have another child. To others the odds of 10 percent sound very high, and they wouldn't dream of having another child. Obviously this is something that each family must decide for themselves. I always back a family's choice, whatever it is, because whatever they choose they are the ones who will have to live with the consequences, and thus it should be solely their choice.

Finally, before leaving the subject of brothers and sisters (and cousins), I want to repeat what I said before when discussing inheritance. Our family studies showed that just because you have a sister, brother, or cousin with autism or Asperger's disorder *you do not* have an increased chance of having a child with a similar disorder. The increased risk (called the recurrence risk estimate) is only for parents who have already had an affected child.

Blind alleys

As the decades of the 1970s, 1980s, and 1990s rolled on there was an explosion of our knowledge of genetics. DNA and RNA, the building blocks of genes, were discovered, and almost daily new techniques were invented to study their structure and how they pass information down from one generation to the next.

Fortunately two world-renowned geneticists were on the UCLA faculty when we were working in Utah, Dr. Robert Sparks and Dr. Anne Spence. They volunteered to join our research team, along with a specialist in genetic immunology, Dr. Reed Warren of Utah.

With their help we conducted studies of gene markers, HLA haplotypes (with the assistance of Professor Terasake at UCLA), segregation analyses, immune system functioning, and others too technical to describe here. Unfortunately none of these research projects shed light on how autism is inherited. Again, lots of work, but no "smoking gun."

As I write this in 2006, several medical centers are extending our initial studies with families that have more than one autistic child (multiple incidence families). They are analyzing genes with new techniques, as I shall describe in a moment, in hopes of discovering the specific abnormalities that cause autism and Asperger's disorder.

The future lies ahead

At least once a week a parent or patient, a student at UCLA, or someone after a lecture somewhere around the world asks the following questions: "So, Dr. Ritvo, what do you really think causes autism and Asperger's disorder? And, why haven't all you doctors and researchers been able to find it after all these years of work?" (That's a pretty direct quote.)

OK, those are fair questions. First I'll tell you why we haven't got the answer yet, that's the easy part. And then I'll give you my best guess as to what it will eventually turn out to be.

The reason we haven't found the answer so far is that we still haven't invented the tools that will let us look in the right place. Remember how I pointed out that Sir Isaac Newton, Copernicus, Darwin, and even Asperger and Kanner made their discoveries by first looking with just their unaided eyes, and then thinking up explanations for what they saw? Well, that is how scientific discoveries start. But we can see only as far as our vision allows. For science to progress we need to invent new tools that improve our vision, that take our power of observation to new levels so that we can see the previously unseeable.

My own scientific attack on the cause of autism and Asperger's disorder stalled in the 1990s, due to our lack of ability to see without the invention of new tools that could look further into our genes. After I discovered all those families with more than one autistic child, and parents who had autism and had autistic kids, it didn't take a rocket scientist to figure out that the cause was most likely to be somewhere in their genes. As I just noted a few paragraphs ago, we tried looking into their genes with all the tools available during the next decade, but unfortunately we couldn't see anything new. Nevertheless, my "best guess" was and still is that the "smoking gun," the cause, in all but the secondary case, will be found in the genes.

There are millions and millions of genes in every cell of our body. They are made up of long strands of chemicals called DNA. These contain the blueprints that direct the construction of our bones, muscles, nerves, and the brain. We pass our genes, our chemical blueprints, on to our children through our eggs and sperm, and they direct the construction of their little bodies.

Now that I am out on the "it's caused by bad genes" limb, let me crawl out on an even shakier branch. Shortly after DNA was discovered we learned to read the "words" it contained (instructions telling the cell what part of the body to make), and it seemed curious that many of the words (strands of DNA) did not appear to contain any useful information. We called these strands or words "junk DNA." Well, nature is much too thrifty to keep DNA with no use around in our genes. The truth of the matter is that we hadn't yet invented the proper tools to read what this part of the DNA did. We were just covering our ignorance by calling it "junk."

But science marches on, and new tools have since been invented that will let us unlock the mysterious meaning of these junk gene words. A brand new fascinating picture is emerging. It turns out that some of these junk genes make cousins of DNA called micro-RNA. These cousins contain timing instructions. They give directions to the construction worker genes, telling them what, where, and when to lay the building blocks of our bodies. They coordinate all the zillion things that have to go on and off at precisely the right time if we are to develop and live successfully.

How can we tie abnormal micro-RNA to the clinical symptoms of autism and Asperger's disorder? I first offered this explanation at a research meeting at the Mt. Saint Hospital in New York City in 2003. This was my "best guess" at that time, and still is. Let's consider just the micro-RNA that directs the growth and connection of brain cells. Let's assume it does not function properly all the time, and thus not all of the parts of the brain can develop on schedule. Rather, some parts get stalled and we get delays of development. Some messages finally get through and we get spurts of development.

Dose this sound familiar to you? Well it does to me, and it would explain all the hallmark symptoms (developmental delays, spurts and plateaus, and separation of the pathways). When the instructions in the micro-RNA are way off, we get severe autism with early symptoms persisting in all the developmental pathways. When the abnormalities are milder and intermittent we get mild/high-functioning autism with spurts and plateaus of development. And finally, when they are mildest, we get later onset and mild symptoms mostly in symbolic language processing and the relatedness problems called "social blindness."

The next few years will be an exciting time for autism research. As I said, I am very optimistic that new tools of genetic analysis will unlock the mysteries of abnormal brain development and zero in on the exact cause. What ultimately makes these micro-RNA genes "go bad"? No one knows yet. Will we be blaming increased radiation (from cosmic rays due to larger holes in the ozone layer, from nuclear reactors, excess X-ray exposure, high-altitude flying, cell phones, radon, or as yet unknown sources of radiation), in vitro fertilization, increased maternal age, hormone treatments, or other things we can't even imagine today?

I can't wait to find out!

Chapter 6

Supportive Treatments: Which Ones, When, and for Whom

Some general points

Recognizing and treating other diseases (if present)

It should go without saying that all children and adults with autism and Asperger's disorder are just as likely to have any other disease as anyone else. Allergies of all types, depression, asthma, celiac disease, lactose intolerance, epilepsy, diabetes schizophrenia, attention deficit disorder, etc. occur in them with exactly the same frequency as they occur in the general population. I am aware that it has often been proposed that autistic children have higher rates of certain allergies and immune system disorders. However, I have not observed this during my decades of evaluating thousands of patients from all corners of the globe. Our research surveys of patients at UCLA and Utah also failed to find evidence of increased allergies or immune system disorders.

Thus it is very important to evaluate autistic kids to make sure they do not have other diseases that require treatment. And we always treat them vigorously, if and when we find them. Just as obvious is the fact that treating their other illnesses does not change the course of their autism or Asperger's disorder. An autistic child who has food allergies deserves to be relieved of the stomachaches caused by certain foods. And while a stomachache-free autistic boy is a much happier boy, he is still an autistic boy. I have to point out this obvious fact because many parents have told me they had hoped their child's autism would improve dramatically if they treated his allergies, for example.

The difference between rational and supportive treatments

When I first described the medical model of disease I explained that there are two general types of treatment. The first, called "rational treatment," is aimed at eliminating the cause of a disease. The second, called "supportive treatment," is aimed at helping Mother Nature do her work. I also said that, unfortunately, and despite our best efforts, we have not yet discovered a rational treatment for autism and Asperger's disorder. Thus we have to rely on nature, and help her as best we can.

But I do not mean to sound pessimistic or fatalistic. As I also described before, these disorders are remittent, they tend to improve by themselves over the course of time. Fortunately, we have developed many supportive treatments that help our patients do the best they possibly can at the stage of brain development they have reached. In this regard we are like tailors. We can't make our patients grow taller, but we can carefully follow their growth and make sure that they "look their best," that is, do the best they can with the skills they have.

The importance of flexibility in treatment plans

Developmental disorders demand flexible treatment plans. Since we are dealing with children whose brains are developing along their own genetically determined unique courses, and we are expecting spurts and plateaus of progress, it is necessary to constantly reassess and be ready to change our plans. What's best at age three may not be best at three and a half. The best school in the autumn may be the wrong one come springtime. What fits an eight-year-old may be wrong for a ten-year-old.

When describing this need to be flexible with parents I frequently compare it to sailing. Having attended a naval academy in high school this comes naturally for me. I explain that helping a child reach his or her maximum potential is like having to sail into the wind to reach home. Since a sailboat can't sail directly into the wind you have to start off on a course that seems closest. Soon you have to reevaluate the wind and tide and tack, or turn in another direction. You keep reevaluating and tacking back and forth till you can finally reach home.

Let's look at the treatment plan for a four-year-old severely autistic child to illustrate this need to tack back and forth. Let's say I find a special education preschool program that is ideal for him, and we start off on tack one. Six month later a reevaluation indicates he has had a spurt in language development and has "outgrown" this school. It's time for tack two. I then find a more appropriate school, but six months later his excellent teacher gets pregnant and leaves. She is replaced with one who has no training or interest in autism. It's time for another reevaluation and to start off on tack three.

By the way, this example gives me the chance to point out why I never recommend a specific school or treatment program without insisting that the parents visit the program before enrolling their child. I have been burned by this happening to me once too often. I recommend to Mrs. Smith that she take her little girl to XYZ School. There she has a wonderful year with Mrs. Green, an experienced teacher. Next year I urge Mrs. Brown to take her little boy to the same school with confidence. Without my knowing it Mrs. Green has moved to Mexico and has been replaced by a woman named Miss Untrained. A few weeks later Mrs. Brown calls me with fire in her voice: "How could you send me there? His teacher is so bad she doesn't know the first thing about teaching autistic children." And I wind up in the doghouse. The lesson is clear. Any service is only as good as the people giving it, and that goes for physicians as well. This is why I always urge parents to visit classrooms and observe diagnostic and treatment sessions. I urge them to let their "gut feeling" as to what is best for their child be the deciding factor in starting and continuing with any professional who is trying to help their child.

Every child and adult with autism and Asperger's disorder needs to be followed by a physician who is knowledgeable about these conditions. Child psychiatrists, child neurologists, and developmental pediatricians most often fill this role. I usually recommend medical and educational reevaluations at least once a year till the teen years, and not so frequently after that. But the need to find the best therapy program for each child at each point in his life never ends.

An early start is best

As with any disorder, the sooner the diagnosis is made and the sooner treatment is started, the better it is. Usually the diagnosis of autism is made by age 36 months, and treatments start then. Asperger's disorder is not usually diagnosed until the relatedness problems caused by "social blindness" interfere with a child's getting along in school, and treatment starts then. Less frequently we will get a call from a wife or husband wondering if their spouse has Asperger's disorder. Even less frequently, an adult will call for a

consultation having read about others who share similar thinking and social relatedness problems, and wondering if he or she has Asperger's
disorder.

While I started this section with the words "an early start is best" I hasten to add that parents should not feel badly or guilty if their child is not
diagnosed at a very early age. These disorders are not like infections that
have to be treated early or they get worse and worse. No, as we have said
over and over, they almost always get better with time. As long as a child is
cared for with love, kindness, and acceptance their brain will continue to
grow along its own genetically determined pathway. We often see severely
and mildly autistic children who were first referred when five, six, or older.
They can also respond very well to our therapies.

Now let's turn our attention to the treatments we prescribe. This will
not be a detailed "how to do it" discussion. Rather, I shall describe the treatments in general terms and give you an idea of when and why we recommend them.

Specific supportive programs and support systems
Behavior therapy
One thing all professionals agree upon today is that autistic children, severe
to mild to high-functioning, need active teaching intervention. Teachers
and therapists must get right in their faces and force relating and participation. Specific goals must be set and ways to best get the child to reach them
put into play. Just letting a child go, observing him, following him around
on the floor, waiting for him to start to learn, being non-directive, in short,
just being passive, does not help. In fact it is counterproductive and can
waste valuable time.

Designing a specific program to get a child to attend, figuring out specific learning goals, and objectively monitoring progress is the name of the
game. This structured part of the child's education process we call "behavior therapy." Other names you may hear it called are "applied behavioral
analysis," "discrete trial training," and older terms like "behavior modification," "operant conditioning," and "aversive therapy."

Behavior therapy has its roots in early studies of classical conditioning
and behavior modification. The first research on autistic children using
these methods was conducted in the 1960s and was aimed at eliminating or
reducing self-injurious repetitive behaviors. "Aversive" methods like yelling
"NO," pinching, slapping, and even mild electric shocks were tried, but
found to have little lasting benefit. Just ignoring bad behaviors and reward-

ing good behaviors was then tried. Candy, smiles, hugs, and kisses proved more effective, and to state the obvious, were a lot more humane. These "warm fuzzy," types of rewards are called "social reinforcers." When such rewards get more of the desired behaviors we are trying to teach we call them "positive social reinforcers." This important technical term is the key to the type of behavior therapy we recommend.

Sometimes we have to start a behavior therapy program with a severely developmentally delayed child by gently directing their actions. These hands-on techniques are called "physical prompts." Once a child gets the idea of how to learn new behaviors we switch to using "social prompts" and rewards (social reinforcers) like hugs, kisses, and saying: "Good work, I love you sooooo much, you are such a good boy!"

Here are the nuts and bolts of how a behavior program works. First, a specially trained "behavior therapist" designs an individual treatment pro gram to suit "Little Alan Anonymous." To accomplish this, he or she reviews Little Alan's development with Mr. and Mrs. Anonymous, observes him at home or at school, and carefully assesses his strengths and weaknesses. Based on this information initial therapy goals are established.

Next a trial teaching situation is set up to figure out which rewards (physical prompts, social reinforcers) work best, and what teaching schedule is best. Some kids can sustain their attention for hours, others for just minutes. After all this information is assembled, the behavior therapist writes out a program for the approval of Mr. and Mrs. Anonymous. If it's OK with them, off they go. If not, it is back to the drawing board till everyone is in agreement. This is a vital step in our opinion, because Mr. and Mrs. A. will have to follow the behavior program when the therapist is not around. If they are not fully "on board" the entire therapy program is doomed to failure.

Finally, the therapist builds in a way to chart little Alan's progress. To return to our sailing analogy, his therapy program has to tack back and forth to keep up with Little Alan's brain development and to make sure he is using all the skills he possesses at any given point in time.

There is a technical term that has become very popular recently, and you should become familiar with it. It is "discrete trial training." This simply refers to a behavior therapy program in with each interaction is recorded separately for subsequent analysis.

As I said at the beginning of our discussion, all professionals agree that structured training is essential. However, there is much controversy as to the number of hours per day and per week that a child should receive behavior therapy. Of course, the answer for a given child depends on the severity of their autism and their ability to benefit. We have observed the results of many programs that have ranged from a maximum of 40+ hours a week to a minimum of one or two hours a week. In general, over the years, it appears that one to three hours a day is the rate that is usually settled upon as best suited to most kids. However, as we said, each child has to be evaluated and have a unique program designed for him, based on his present level of functioning, his potential, and his response to a trial of therapy.

There has also been much controversy among experts in the field of behavior therapy and special education as to what long-term treatment goals to expect. Some early reports used words like "recovery" and "normalization" when describing their results. Unfortunately, these claims have not withstood the test of time. There is no treatment that has been shown to result in "recovery," or "cure" in the usual meaning of these terms. Rather, it is generally agreed upon now that behavior therapy is the best way to help an autistic child to utilize the skills that he or she has, and to maximize their potential. And it is also generally agreed that every young autistic child should be evaluated to determine if behavior therapy could be helpful, as it most likely will be.

Special education programs

Fortunately, the heroic efforts of parents and professionals who lobbied to obtain appropriate education for autistic children during the 1970s and 1980s has paid off in a big way. In those early years autistic kids were usually dumped into overcrowded classes with "mentally retarded," or obviously brain damaged, or seriously emotionally disturbed kids, if they were even allowed to attend public school. Today it is the responsibility of every school district in the United States, and many other countries, to provide "an appropriate education, in the least restricted environment, as close to their home as possible." I had many exciting times lobbying before Congress and state governments assisting parents to get the passage of such legislation as Federal PL 94–142 which contains those words.

Today every autistic child in the United States is entitled by law to receive a complete evaluation by the special education department of their school district, and as soon as they are old enough to enter. This is usually at the preschool level, age four to five years. Specially trained professionals in the areas of special education, psychology, occupational therapy, speech and language therapy, physical therapy, and behavior therapy should participate in the evaluation. Written reports and recommendations should be given to the parents. And there should be a process for review and appeal available if the parents don't agree with the school district's recommendations for their child.

Each school district should be able to provide all the therapies needed for each autistic child within their district. If not, they should purchase appropriate educational support from private vendors. Some school districts have full-time advocates to assist parents. I also know professionals who serve as advocates to help parents find a proper placement for their child. I often work with such specialists. Here are some guidelines of what to look for and what to expect from an ideal special education program.

1. A teacher specially trained and experienced in teaching autistic children should be in charge of the class. That goes without saying, but as the old saying goes, unfortunately "What should be often ain't."

2. The school district should provide a special education plan designed for each child. These are called IEPs (individual education programs). There should be appropriate monitoring of each student's progress with periodic feedback for their parents built in. There are several specific special education programs for autistic children that have proven their worth over the years. Our friends Dr. Eric Schopler and Dr. Bob Reichler developed our favorite in North Carolina. It is called the TEACCH program (Teaching and Education of Autistic and related Communication handicapped CHildren). It combines elements of behavior therapy and less formally structured activities into a carefully designed curriculum that covers the entire school day. Careful monitoring of progress and increasing goals are spelled out. We frequently advise parents to see if a TEACCH-based classroom is available nearby.

3. An individual behavior therapy program for each student should be built into their school day. This program should be designed by behavior specialists and administered by trained therapists or teachers trained to provide behavior therapy.

4. Each child in a special education classroom should be allowed to attend regular classrooms for as much of the school day as is appropriate. This is referred to as "mainstreaming" and is always beneficial, both for autistic children and non-autistic children. Mainstreaming, like any other program or therapy, can be overdone. When parents insist on mainstreaming their child more

than is appropriate (something that has happened too often), I ask them this simple question. If your child could not swim would you want the teacher to throw him in the deep end of the pool, or keep him at the shallow end till he learned how? This usually dampens their enthusiasm for mainstreaming when it is not appropriate.

5.   The special education program should run all year to prevent regressions.

6.   Occupational therapy, physical therapy, and speech and language therapy evaluations should be conducted, and therapy offered if indicated.

7.   Shadow teachers, professional teachers' aides, and non-autistic student aides should be used when indicated. They are able to provide social support, help keep a child on task, and allow for smooth transitions from one activity or classroom to another. We always encourage their use when indicated.

8.   Special transportation is usually provided by the school district, and should be requested.

Medications

The first thing I must do before discussing medication is give you a warning. Autistic children, like all children, are subject to sensitivity and allergic reactions, side effects, paradoxical responses, and other weird and unpredictable things when given any type of medication. To complicate matters further, hardly any of our medications have been evaluated in children before being put on the market. The Food and Drug Administration (FDA) has only recently required special studies of medications prescribed for children, so it is a *caveat emptor* situation – buyer beware!

I have had as much experience as anyone with medication in these disorders, and I am always very, very, cautious. That said, I only prescribe medications when they are clearly indicated, and then only on a trial basis. I always start with very small doses, and increase the dose only after I am sure that there are no bad side effects. Sometimes a tenth or a quarter of a dose proves sufficient!

The most frequent request I get for medication is when an autistic child is overactive and in danger of hurting himself or others. When a chemical "straitjacket" is needed, to put it bluntly, I prescribe sedative-type tranquilizer medications. I like to start these drugs in the hospital, if possible. I start with a very small dose and increase the amount gradually after two or three days until the child is calmed down and controllable. Then, after no longer than one or two weeks, I start to taper the dose at the same rate, and discontinue it over a week or two. In the vast majority of cases this proves effective and the child remains calmed down and manageable. Rarely a second course for a few weeks is required. Let me stress again, I only resort to sedative-type medications in extreme situations, and when all other non-medication methods have failed.

The second most frequent request I get is for anti-anxiety or anti-depressant medications to help calm a very anxious, very obsessive, or very depressed autistic child. Only one or two of the anti-anxiety and anti-depressant medications approved for adults have been evaluated in children. Thus, each parent will have to find a doctor who will carefully monitor these medications in order to find one that works for their child. Again, I always start with a very small dose, gradually increase it till I see a desired effect, and then taper it after two or three months.

Another frequent request for medication comes if it appears that an autistic child also has attention deficit hyperactivity disorder (ADHD). Since this disorder occurs in approximately 3–4 percent of all boys, any autistic boy has a similar percentage chance of also having ADHD. In order to confirm a diagnosis I review the child's history with this in mind. If it seems likely that ADHD is present I may, please note I stress the word *may*, conduct a one-day trial with a stimulant medication to see if we get a para-doxical response. (If the stimulant medication decreases hyperactivity it is called paradoxical because stimulants "speed up" normal children.) A para-doxical reaction tends to confirm the diagnosis. Such medication trials should be conducted only under the direction of a physician specially trained in diagnosing and treating ADHD. Properly treating ADHD when it exists along with autism is crucial, as untreated ADHD can sabotage all our other treatment efforts.

Occupational therapy

The application of occupational therapy (OT) techniques for autism were pioneered in the 1960s by Dr. Jean Ayres, the founder of Sensory Integra-tion Therapy. She and her students were searching for a way to understand and treat the sensory-motor symptoms, particularly those involving the position, vestibular and tactile systems.

In those years I was studying the same problems and had the privilege of meeting and working with her. One thing I shall never forget is how she always built "fun factors" into her treatment sessions. It was always hard to tell who was enjoying the treatment sessions more, Dr. Ayres or her autistic patients! Her husband was an architect who designed and built special equipment for her clinic. When I asked her one day why she didn't patent this special equipment she said, "Oh I couldn't do that, it is my gift to the children." Her theoretical formulations led to very specific treatments, and her special equipment is still used worldwide today.

Over the past decades OT for autism and Asperger's disorder has evolved into three separate areas, sensory integration treatment, gross and fine motor treatment, and play and socialization treatment. I shall describe each separately, although they are usually administered in the same clinical setting.

Sensory integration therapy

This treatment assists a child in organizing and processing sensory information. Many children over- and/or underrespond to sensory inputs. This limits their ability to interact in a purposeful way. Sensory Integration Therapy teaches the child to compensate for the effects of developmental delays in the parts of the brain that modulate or regulate the intensity of incoming sensations. For example, many autistic children are afraid of heights, some love to spin while others fear that motion. Some children will stay on swings all day while others fear them. All of these sensory symptoms are addressed in Sensory Integration Therapy sessions.

The therapist uses specialized gym-like equipment; each piece is designed to address a specific sensory problem. The child gradually learns to master fears. Other sensory symptoms addressed can be over- or undersensitivity to touch and pain. Brushing and other such techniques, which are graduated in intensity and frequency, are employed to desensitize kids who over- or underreact to sound, temperature, smell, and taste.

Many sensory integration clinics ressemble children's gyms; however, treatment can be carried out in a variety of settings including home and school. The therapist meets the child where he or she is at, slowly introducing "just the right amount of sensory stimulation," guiding and prompting every movement at every moment.

Gross motor and fine motor treatment

Thought not too common, some autistic children experience delays in developing "gross motor skills" (walking, running, skipping, jumping, coordinating actions). For them, special gym equipment is also utilized under the watchful eye of the occupational therapist. Their progress is carefully monitored to match their improving skill level in order to prevent undue anxiety or injury as new skills are learned.

Developmental delays of fine motor skills (grasping a pencil or spoon correctly, getting the fork into the mouth instead of the ear, buttoning clothes and tying shoes) frequently occur. Occupational therapists design special programs and create one-of-a-kind tools to help their autistic patients master such intricate tasks one step at a time. This calls for much creativity and is very challenging, and is what makes this profession so rewarding.

Play and socialization treatment

This is a relatively new field of specialization within the profession of occupational therapy. It is a natural outgrowing of the classical role of the occupational therapist's teaching daily living skills to developmentally delayed and neurologically handicapped children. It stems from the ever-increasing numbers of mildly autistic and Asperger's disorder children that have recently come to our attention. These children need therapy to develop appropriate play skills and appropriate social skills.

With this therapy, language delays (concrete thinking, difficulty assigning symbolic meaning), and relatedness delays (social blindness, needing to remain aloof, fear of intimacy) are treated in small groups of three to six children. The groups can contain both boys and girls, and non-autistic children are frequently invited to attend. Under close supervision age-appropriate group games such as Monopoly, card games, and construction projects proceed with a focus on teaching the ability to perform cooperative actions. Sharing space, equipment, ideas, and leadership roles are all crucial topics. The therapist identifies and explains feeling such as jealousy, rage, frustration, empathy, and the need to imagine how others are feeling. The goals include learning social awareness, how to read social cues, how to feel comfortable and competent in social situations, and new ways of thinking about themselves and others.

For teenagers, mock dates, eating in restaurants, getting crushed at rock concerts, attending school sports and similar social events are built into therapy "outings." Sex education, including such topics as puberty, menstruation, masturbation, homosexuality, birth control, venereal disease, pornography, etc., is important for these children to discuss, as it is for all teenagers. Obviously the therapist needs to obtain prior parental consent and understanding.

Occupational therapists also conduct various types of "social skills" groups for adults with mild autism or Asperger's disorder. Some groups are just for married couples. These are usually very helpful to both partners. The one with Asperger's disorder gets to learn to understand their thinking style better, to read social cues, be more empathetic, and how to read emotional reactions. The other partner gains an appreciation for the handicaps and social adjustment difficulties of their partner. Here, as I described before, the therapist often makes home visits and shares real-life experiences, while commenting on appropriate feelings and acting as a translator for social cues.

To repeat, the goals of these therapies whether with kids, teenagers, or adults are the same. First recognition of social cues must be learned. Recognizing the meaning of gestures or tone of voice, knowing how close to stand, the pacing and spacing of verbal responses, and taking turns in conversation just don't come naturally. Next, repeated practice is essential. Finally, providing insight and giving positive feedback sets the stage for long-lasting benefits.

Speech and language therapy

Every young child who is diagnosed with severe or mild/high-functioning autism should be evaluated by a speech and language therapist to see if treatment in one or both of these areas could help. The testing consists of reviewing the history with the parents and having a friendly, play-type interview with the child. During this interview the child's level of speech and language development are objectively determined, as well as the best ways of communicating with the child.

Speech therapy is recommended when a child has difficulty coordinating the muscles that produce speech. It usually consists of individual or group sessions, teaching how to make proper sounds by imitation and repetition. Also, special techniques may be used, such as breaking words down into sound bits and patterns they can learn correctly one at a time, and then putting them together to form words. This is very specialized work, and requires a licensed therapist who is trained to work with autistic children to be most successful.

Language therapy focuses on helping autistic children as they move along the language/cognitive developmental pathway that I described in detail before. The therapist determines where the child is delayed and designs ways of communicating at that level. They use many non-verbal techniques ranging from pointing at pictures, simplified sign language, and drawing and writing. With older autistic children and those with Asperger's disorder they focus on helping the child understand symbolic meaning, and understanding and expressing complex thoughts. They have to be very creative and work closely with parents and teachers so that the child can communicate in similar ways when they are at home or at school.

Speech and language therapists closely watch for spurts of brain development. When these occur, more mature ways of communicating become possible, and they have to teach the child how to use them. For example, a little girl with severe autism I know moved from just being able to use simple sign language, to pointing to letters, and then to reading words in just a few months. Her therapist kept pace with her spurt in brain development, and moved her young patient up the developmental ladder as fast as she could go. Moving ahead too fast leads to frustration and failure and must always be guarded against.

Supportive cognitive psychotherapy and life skills coaching

I have been often asked if psychoanalysis is indicated for those with very mild/high-functioning autism and Asperger's disorder. Having had extensive training in this area I am in a position to answer. And my answer is "NO." I have never run into a case where it has proved helpful, and I have never recommended it myself. I say this being fully aware that there are many psychoanalysts and psychotherapists especially in the United States, Britain, France, and South America who still believe that autism and Asperger's disorder occur in those with normal brain development and were "psychologically poisoned" by their parents. Based on this old theory they recommend psychoanalysis. As you know from having read this far, there is overwhelming scientific evidence that this is simply not true. Autism and Asperger's disorder result from abnormal brain development, period. Good, bad, or indifferent parenting has nothing to do with causing it. Therefore any treatment aimed at uncovering childhood memories and repairing presumed psychic damage is not only not indicated, it would just waste valuable time and money, and is possibly harmful.

Traditional psychotherapy aimed at providing insight into unconscious motivation has, in my experience, been of little value for those with autism and Asperger's disorder. Rather, I recommend life skills coaching which is usually very helpful. This involves teaching skills on how to get along in life and giving direct advice. A wide variety of professionals can fulfill this role, and a psychiatrist or other medical doctor is rarely required unless medications are part of the therapy.

I have had good luck holding family conferences with parents, siblings, and their autistic child when a crisis arises. There are professionals who specialize in working with families, and I often recommend them when communication breaks down and an objective referee is needed to restore peace and understanding.

School counselors, rabbis and ministers, little league coaches, and uncles and aunts can make good "coaches" for kids with autism and Asperger's disorder. Being one step removed from their parents, they are more likely to be listened to.

Vocational training

Experts in vocational training are a vital part of our treatment team. They usually enter the lives of those with mild/high-functioning autism and Asperger's disorder in their late teen years, after high school or college. While some are in private practice, most work with charitable, state, or federal agencies. Their function is straightforward. They start out with a careful assessment of a person's emotional, intellectual, and physical skills, strengths, weaknesses, and wishes. Then they recommend what to look for on the job market, and help them find it.

Those with severe symptoms are usually directed to sheltered or supervised work settings. Those with mild symptoms are directed to jobs that are in keeping with their interests, their level of language processing, and their level of social relatedness. One young man in the severe category I know is a ground keeper at his church, another is a cab driver, another works for a bus company doing routine maintenance tasks, another is a cashier at a movie house, several work on farms, another is a supervisor at a workshop for physically disabled adults, and so on. Jobs with daily or weekly routines, repetitive functions, and limited contact with the public are usually best for those whose obvious symptoms persist into adulthood.

Those autistics with mild symptoms and those with Asperger's disorder usually do not seek the help of vocational counselors. They can do almost everything anyone else can do. I know many who are doctors, lawyers, successful businessmen, accountants, and teachers (including two college professors), bus drivers, cooks, and members of the armed services. Many are married and have children. Others I know live solitary lives with little need for friends or social relationships of any sort. In summary, if they have very mild symptoms, they can blend into society without notice or need for help.

Supported living and estate planning

It is best to start making long-range plans once a loved one reaches 21. Developmental spurts rarely occur past this age, and the late teens and early twenties are natural times for kids to move away from home.

There are generally two types of "supportive living" available. First, there are "group homes" in which several young adults share a home or apartment and have full-time live-in supervision. The second consists of a house or apartment in which two or three "housemates" live with part-time non-live-in supervision. Depending on the severity of a person's symptoms and their parents' preferences, I have seen both types work well.

Often brothers, sisters, relatives, or friends agree to take on long-term living-in commitments. This may work out for a while, but the autistic person may outlive these caretakers, and plans for this happening must be made well in advance.

If supported living is being considered, I recommend parents begin by contacting the local chapter of their autism society or other support groups. By getting in touch with other parents who have crossed this bridge they can get a feel for what is available and what has worked best near where they live. Unfortunately there are no "Consumer Reports" or other quality-control measures available. You will have to go on personal recommendations, make many visits, and ultimately do what your heart tells you is best.

Estate planning must also be considered when making long-range plans. Fortunately there are attorneys who specialize in estate planning for developmentally disabled individuals, and you can find them by contacting your local attorneys' association, which is listed in your phone book.

Sports and hobbies

Sports and hobbies, when properly chosen and properly monitored, can be wonderful therapeutic activities for kids with autism and Asperger's disorder. The wrong ones, or if not properly supervised, can be roads to lower self-esteem, further isolation, and emotional pain.

Here are some guidelines to consider when choosing sports and hobbies:

1. First and foremost, always inform teachers, coaches, and other supervisors of your child's special needs (and their diagnosis if that would be helpful) when they first join a group activity, special school, or club. If the people in charge are not immediately understanding and empathetic, leave at once, and don't waste your time trying to educate them. We want our kids to be only with

adults who are loving, kind, patient, and want to have happy children in their care. "Winning a gold medal" is not our goal. Learning a skill, learning to get along in a group, gaining self-confidence, and having fun are the only goals of sports and hobbies that these kids need.

2.   Pick sports and activities where your child is competing only against himself or herself. Team sports such a baseball are recipes for disaster. (There are at least 20 others with pairs of eyes watching the frightened batter maybe striking out, or trying to catch and maybe dropping a ball – all ready to yell "Boo, we lost because of you!" – Too much stress.) When there are teammates counting on you, hostility and scapegoating are always lurking nearby.

Non-competitive, non-team activities like gymnastics, dancing, horseback riding, swimming, bowling, camping, hiking, biking, ice skating, snow skiing or snowboarding, water skiing, sailing, and fly fishing are all examples of sports that can improve physical coordination and teach getting along with instructors and other kids (in parallel) who are also learning at the same time. They can all be done without the stress of having to "win" anything. I am sure you can easily add dozens more non-competitive activities to this list.

Joining a theater group where everyone gets a part (no "try out" anxiety) can be particularly therapeutic in helping to develop social skills. Playing a part of another person fosters symbolic thinking by showing how to shift between being yourself and playing someone else in the show. Drama coaches thus can make great "therapists." As I said above, it is best if they are told of a child's diagnosis up front, and their help and understanding enlisted from the beginning. If they don't want to help and prefer to place the play first – just say "Thank you and good bye."

The one sport that I recommend most often for boys and girls from age four on up is martial arts. My youngest son Max started when he was four and I recall with a warm smile how we all clapped when he was finally able to stand on one little foot for at least three seconds. Now, nine years later, he has earned an advanced black belt and has excellent coordination, a strong healthy physique, lots of self-esteem, and great values.

Here are some of the therapeutic benefits of this sport. The martial arts teachers, and other non-regular school teachers, are the only ones a child keeps working with year after year. Each class begins with a bow of respect to the teacher and ends with a brief lecture on the principles of Black Belt.

These include honesty, humility, compassion, courage, devotion, harmony, grace, self-discipline, respect for others, wisdom, and indomitable spirit. Can you imagine better social skills training? Do you see why I have prescribed this "medication" for dozens of kids with high-functioning autism and Asperger's disorder?

And I advise parents to be sure to find a martial arts studio run by a mature dedicated professional whose spiritual values they respect. And let the teacher know their child's diagnosis right away and their goals for their child's development, and that the focus remains on their having "fun" while they learn to master their bodies, improve their mental focus, learn good social values, socialize, and develop self-confidence.

There are many other similar "therapeutic" non-academic schools, classes, and activities where a child can learn social skills in non-competitive settings under the direction of understanding adults. Now you know the ingredients I am recommending, look around your neighborhood and I'm sure you'll find more than one that is suitable for your child.

Hobbies offer the same opportunity for your child to have fun while learning social skills. But beware; once one is found do not let it dominate your child's time and thoughts. There is a tendency for autistic and Asperger's kids to get perseverative or overinvolved in certain activities and interests. I recall a lad who got so hooked on chess that it was all he thought about all day and he dreamed up games in his sleep. As in all of life, too much of a good thing will turn it into a bad thing. With this warning, try to find a hobby that involves group activity but is not competitive. Going to hobby shows, collectors' exhibitions, and hobby classes offer excellent opportunities for social skills learning while having fun.

Helping non-affected brothers and sisters

Non-autistic siblings are "built-in" social skills therapists for their autistic brothers and sisters. They can provide role models, companionship, and unequivocal love and acceptance.

I am often asked what is the long-term impact on the other kids in the family of having an autistic brother or sister? I have found that the non-autistic siblings of my patients generally grow up to be very loving, caring adults with generous spirits. While I have no statistics to back this up, it seems more of them than expected choose health care and teaching careers. I hear over and over from them that they learned early that life is not fair, and that giving care is rewarding in and of itself. They all say that it was important that they had an explanation of their sibling's condition as soon as they were old enough to realize there were differences. This generally occurred when they reached elementary school age, about five or six at the latest.

Mrs. Ilana Katz is the loving mother of a boy I diagnosed as having autism many years ago. She brought to my attention the importance of being sensitive to the impact of autism and Asperger's disorder on brothers and sisters, and the need to do something about it. We discussed this issue at great length and focused on a problem that confronts every parent with young non-autistic children: how do you explain autism to them? After much thought and research Ilana proposed our writing a book on this subject, and the result was *Joey and Sam*. This little picturebook never made the *New York Times* bestseller list, but is a perennial bestseller with parents of autistic and Asperger's disorder children. It explains in simple words and lovely pictures what autism is and how it affects the lives of two little boys, Joey and Sam, one of whom has autism. I recommend it without hesitation (and with complete objectivity).

Unproven theories about the causes of autism, and treatments to avoid

Before we leave this chapter I want to let you know about some old theories of what causes autism and some of the treatments they led to. In my medical opinion, based on my decades of experience and continuing daily to review the relevant scientific literature, I can assure you that the following theories are unproven and ineffective:

Here are some of the treatments I advise parents against because they have yet to be scientifically proven, they needlessly squander limited family

- bad parenting
- leaky guts
- brain allergies
- yeast infections

- celiac disorders
- mercury poisoning
- thiomeresol poisoning
- mal-learning.

resources, and they give vulnerable parents false hope of a cure (which I pray we will one day have). However, the following treatments are not harmful or dangerous:

- auditory integration training
- facilitated communication
- colored lens treatment
- gluten and casein free diets

- mega doses of vitamins
- the Son-Rise program
- REI therapy program

Still other treatments, I firmly believe, should never be given to autistic or Asperger's patients because they are not only unproven, but also can have dangerous side effects. These include the following treatments:

- nystatin treatment
- chelation
- immunoglobulin therapy
- steroids

- painful aversive therapy
- cranial-cervical spinal manipulation

The tragedy of not vaccinating infants

One disproved theory of causation deserves special mention because of the harm it has caused, and is still unfortunately causing. It had been suggested that a mercury-based preservative that was used in vaccines (it is no longer used) could injure the brain and thus cause secondary autism. This theory came about because many autistic children first show symptoms at about 18 months of age, just after receiving their "shots."

Several research studies in the United States, Europe, and Japan have failed to find any evidence that vaccinations are linked to autism. In those rare cases where children have had serious reactions to a vaccination and brain damage has occurred, autism is not the result. These children look and act very differently from autistics. The National Institute of Health recently released a report that is available online (www.pubmed-central.nih.gov) for anyone who is particularly interested in reviewing all the information available on this subject. Whether a mercury preservative was involved or not is a moot point now, because, as I noted above, it has been removed from all vaccines now being manufactured.

Now for the danger I mentioned this theory has caused. Over the past few years some parents became scared and refused to have their infants and toddlers vaccinated. These infants and toddlers remained at risk for very serious infections and permanent brain damage from measles, chickenpox, mumps, and other viruses that can infect the brain. These are diseases that fortunately our modern vaccines can easily prevent. And here is the saddest part. I recently read a report from Ireland of increase in measles encephalitis (permanent brain damage) in infants during the past year. These infants were the ones left unprotected because their parents had been needlessly frightened and did not have them vaccinated.

The bottom line, in my opinion, and in the opinion of the mainstream medical community is that all children should receive all the vaccinations recommended by their doctors, in accordance with the guidelines of the American Medical Association and the American Academy of Pediatrics (or similar authoritative professional agencies in your country of residence).

A final word about another suggested, and as yet untested theory, namely that giving them too many vaccinations at the same time can possibly overwhelm a child's immune system and cause problems. For those who want to avoid this possibility I advise you to ask your doctor to spread out your child's vaccinations over a period of time, but make sure all are given.

Common sense dictates that we must all work together to avoid the return of deadly epidemics that are easily preventable, thanks to modern medical science.

Chapter 7

My Casebook

This chapter is arranged in two sections. First you will find detailed life stories of eight children and adults. Each one is a composite of actual patients of mine, and their stories are just as I learned them when we were working together. Their lives poignantly show the many ways autism and Asperger's disorder can appear, can masquerade as other disorders, and can change over a lifetime. Obviously their names and other identifying factors have been changed to respect their privacy.

At the end of each story you will find a sentence inviting you make your own diagnosis and prognosis (outcome predictions). This gives you a chance to come to your own conclusions as to their exact diagnoses and predictions about their future. Then you will find my diagnoses and predictions. Maybe you won't agree with me. (And you are perfectly entitled not to!)

The second section contains brief "thumbnail" descriptions of 14 parents who have autism or Asperger's disorder. We met because their autistic children were my patients, not because they came for help themselves. For this reason I could not use them to draw conclusions about the genetic transmission of autism in general. However, it's just common sense to conclude that at least in these families the "dice were loaded." This is because autism is so rare the odds of it occurring in two generations by chance are very, very remote.

Children and adults with autism or Asperger's disorder

Alistair

If you are ever in Washington, DC, and if you ever take a taxi, and if you happen to get Mr. A for a driver you will be a very lucky passenger. You will be greeted courteously; you will ride in peace and quiet, undisturbed by needless chitchat from the driver. You will be taken to your destination by the shortest route, in the quickest time depending on the traffic, and you will be charged the correct fare. No, you will not be in a futuristic cab driven by a robot, you will be in a regular cab driven by a young man who was my patient some years ago!

At the outset of our first diagnostic interview Alistair's mother told me:

> He started talking rather later than his sister, not till he was almost four. Then he repeated every TV show and movie he saw in perfect tone and rhythm till he was almost six. Then he suddenly began to speak almost normally except for a singsong tone. When he was about five he fell in love with all kinds of maps and pictures of the stars. He memorized really complicated star charts and street maps with amazing ease. We started him in school late because he was so late talking. He was tested and they called him dyslexic, but he moved through high school with average grades. His teachers often told me that he could "memorize everything." He never enjoyed sports and he never had a girlfriend or went to a dance in high school. He was happy to spend his time by himself with his hobbies.

He was still interested in maps and star charts when I met him at age 24. A family member got him a job driving a cab after he graduated from high school and he had been a model employee for three years.

Alistair was born after a normal pregnancy and delivery. He had no relatives with autism or other developmental delays and had always been in excellent physical health. He never had a true "friend or pal," but knew "lots of kids in elementary school and high school." In fact, he could recite the names of everyone in his school, grouped by class, yet he never had a sleepover, went to a party, or had a date. He was always content to "get along and be left alone" (his words). When I asked him about his sexual development he said, in an offhand manner with no hint of guilt, shame, or anxiety: "I discovered masturbation by accident when I was about 16, and if I get feeling funny down there I know what to do to make myself feel good, and not feel funny any more."

When we met he was living alone in a one-bedroom apartment. He earned enough money driving his cab to pay all his bills, have some left over to go to the movies, which he did religiously each weekend, and "to save for my future when mom and dad are gone." He visited his parents and sister on a regular schedule, but otherwise was content to be alone when not working. He liked to read mystery books and keep elaborate schedules of his daily routines and his cab driving. He had a detailed street map of Washington, DC and the surrounding area in his head.

Between ages two and seven he was said to have flapped his hands before his eyes for hours at a time, to have loved to spin things and watch a record player for hours, to have been frightened by loud noises, such as the vacuum cleaner, and to have gone out in the winter without a coat unless reminded. All these behaviors suddenly decreased between ages seven and eight but persisted into adulthood on very rare occasions.

His parents were worried about his not being able to get along with other kids and took him to a psychiatrist when he was nine. They were told his diagnosis was primary autism and that there was no treatment for this "type of retardation." (Remember, this was in the 1980s.) He struggled through public school with no help, managed to graduate high school, and then started driving his cab.

When last I saw him he was 26 years old. He still used a few echoic phrases, had stilted social mannerisms, but his demeanor was always correct. He was very cooperative in donating blood for my genetic studies, telling me: "So I can help people with autism, people like me."

What is your diagnosis? What is your prognosis?

Here are my thoughts:

Alistair had plateaus and major spurts of development at age six, with other minor spurts after that. He showed separation of his sensory-motor, language, and relatedness developmental pathways that are typical of autism. He had many sensory-motor symptoms when young, and some minor ones persist to adulthood. The overall level of his social development places him in the diagnostic category of mild high-functioning adult autism. This is because he has mild but persistent symptoms of language processing (concrete thinking, perseverative interests), relatedness problems (no true friends, no interest in interacting with others, social aloofness), and some persistent sensory-motor repetitive behaviors (hand flapping). His strengths are his feelings of self-confidence and his mature independent living skills (he lives on his own, has financial independence – he earns his own living and manages his money on his own).

My prognosis is that he will change little as he gets older. He will continue to be self-supporting and may even find a long-term "caretaking" type of relationship with a woman who falls in love with him, and marries him. I have many other patients with his degree of severity of autism who are married. A further plus for him is the continued acceptance and support of his family.

Susan

A pediatrician referred this beautiful curly-haired little girl to me when she was five and a half years old. She arrived with two diagnoses: severe mental retardation and epilepsy (seizures).

Susan's mother told me that she had a cousin on her mother's side who had autism, but otherwise both she and her husband's family histories were unremarkable. Susan was a wanted and loved child who was born after a normal pregnancy and delivery. She had been in good physical health, had all her "shots," and passed all her motor milestones (sitting, walking, running, jumping, climbing) at the expected times. When she was twelve months old she was thought to be deaf because she did not respond to certain noises, but ambient hearing tests were normal. Since she would respond to her favorite TV theme songs from another room her parents stopped worrying about her hearing. Although Susan was slow starting to talk she had always made her needs known with gestures or by pulling someone by the hand. From age two on she was interested in the TV, record players, and other electric appliances, which she could take apart and re-assemble with ease. She always kept her things in neat order and lined her toys up, fussing if things were missing or out of order. She had very specific food preferences and spit out lumpy foods as she did not like to chew. At four she suddenly started using single words to label things, and "suddenly toilet trained herself."

Susan had a habit of falling on the floor, kicking her feet rhythmically, and staring at the ceiling for a few moments during which she seemed to be "out of touch." These episodes started when she was about two and a half and were continuing once or twice a month when I saw her. Sometimes she would lie on the floor and flap her hands before or after one of these spells for up to a half hour. Her pediatrician thought these could be epileptic seizures and an EEG was obtained when she was three and a half. It was read as showing "Diffuse Slowing, No Seizure Focus Seen." Susan was placed on two anti-seizure medications with no change in her "spells" over the next six months, and then they were stopped. Over the next year Susan's mother tried a variety of diets, chelating, megavitamins, and herbal remedies – all to no avail, so she stopped these too.

When Susan was brought to preschool at age four and a half her parents were told bluntly after a one-hour "complete evaluation" that she was brain damaged and mentally retarded. The school psychologist was completely convinced that her future was very poor. Susan's mother, to the best of her recollection, was told:

> She will need to be in special programs for the very retarded while in school, and then live in a place for the mentally incompetent for the rest of her life. Since she speaks so little, intelligence tests are useless, and they would only prove that she is in the profound category. There is no treatment for these low-level children and you need to face the reality of her being retarded all her life. She will never be able to become a member of your family.

Fortunately, Susan's pediatrician did not buy these conclusions. Instead he discussed her case with a colleague who suggested referring her to me at UCLA for a second opinion.

What is your diagnosis? What is your prognosis?

Here are my thoughts:

After reviewing Susan's developmental history and interviewing her, it quickly became apparent that she had developmental spurts and delays, and separation of her developmental pathways. Her gross and fine motor skills were at the age-appropriate levels. Her "seizures" were typical of the repetitive sensory-motor behaviors we see frequently in autism. Her language delay was primarily in the expressive area. She knew a lot of things and could do a lot of things that told me she was in no way mentally retarded. And lastly, the way she related to me and to her parents was very typical of a child with a developmental delay in this area, not a child who was mentally retarded. Specifically, she did not use eye contact, used others as extensions of herself by taking their hand to obtain things, used objects as she wanted, not as they were designed to be used, and showed infantile attachment and signs of affection to others typical of severely autistic children.

My diagnosis of Susan was "autistic disorder, severe form." I assured her parents that there was no need to worry about epilepsy, and "mental retardation" was a term they could forget about. (I also discussed the diagnosis extensively with her pediatrician and school psychologist.)

When discussing the prognosis with her parents I pointed out the strong probability that Susan would have developmental spurts in the months and years ahead. Since she was only five and a half, many years of potential brain growth lay ahead, and it would be unfair to her to make any long-term predictions at this time. We set out a treatment program of behavior therapy, special education, speech and language therapy, and occupational therapy. We left it that I would see her again in three months' time to see what progress she had made. They left relieved to have found out that she did not have a seizure disorder, was not retarded, and that there was a good possibility that she would have developmental spurts ahead.

Brad

I first learned about Brad at a Christmas party. His parents were friends of friends of mine and they sought me out when they heard I was a "child shrink." Over egg nog the told me that their son, Brad, was being threat-ened with expulsion from his special education school. He was in an SED class (for the Seriously Emotionally Disturbed) and was "uncontrollably acting out his hostility." He had been at this school for many years and it had an excellent reputation.

They rushed to explain that Brad had not begun speaking till he was almost eight years old and been diagnosed by several doctors and psycho-logists as being "moderately mentally retarded and emotionally disturbed." Now, at age eleven Brad was a big aggressive boy who would not behave at school, was picking up new bad behaviors from his classmates every day, and was about to be expelled. Did I have any suggestions? "Yes," I said. "Let's do a complete evaluation and see where it leads us."

Brad's developmental history was interesting. His medical and family history, and his mother's pregnancy gave no clues as to why he was "retarded." True he did not speak till he was almost eight, true he was tested several times and scored in the severe to moderate mental retardation range, and true he required 24-hour supervision all his life. Not true that he was "retarded" in all areas. Before he could talk he learned to care for many of his personal hygiene needs. He made his wishes known by gestures, by leading others by the hand, by drawing crude pictures, and by making things for himself in the kitchen. He could take apart complicated house-hold items and put them back together, and he was very aware of where he was when in the car. He also spent many hours playing complicated video games. When he did start to talk he began by repeating what he heard. "Like he had a tape recorder in his head," his mother remembered. His voice was loud and he lacked appropriate inflections for a long time. From ages two to six he had many repetitive habits, such as body rocking, jumping up and down in one place for long periods, flapping his hands in front of his eyes, and shaking sticks and pencils in his hands. He still did some of these things when I met him. And his favorite toy was a trampoline.

Brad had been in classes for emotionally disturbed students since starting school and recently had learned many bad words, bad behaviors, and bad habits. His language consisted mostly of repeating what he heard, and the rest consisted of very concrete statements labeling things or stating what he wanted.

Brad never looked directly at me during my diagnostic interview, and only acknowledged me when I asked him to give me his video game. "No you don't get it, it's mine," he shouted, and continued to play. This was the most interaction I got over an hour's time.

What is your diagnosis? What is your prognosis?

Here are my thoughts:

In retrospect it was clear that Brad had all the developmental delays, spurts, separation of developmental pathways, and behaviors typical of autism. Up to the point he started to talk he could have been in the severe category, but at age eight he began to have developmental spurts which allowed me to move him up to the mild/high-functioning category.

I am happy to say that once it was recognized that Brad had autism his parents began an extensive and appropriate treatment plan. A behavior therapist designed a program that was carried out initially at home. He also started speech and language therapy. And just as important, he was placed in a classroom for autistic students with a behavior-therapy based curriculum. He quickly gave up the aggressive behaviors he was learning from his emotionally disturbed ex-classmates and adopted socially appropriate behaviors which were "taught" as part of his behavior therapy curriculum.

As the years went by (he is now in his early thirties) Brad developed many new skills. There were periods when he required mild sedative-type medications to help him adjust to increasing social pressures to comply with rules he did not fully understand. At I write this, he is living in an apartment with an autistic roommate. They are monitored by a social worker who visits them twice a week. He has a job five days a week at a sheltered workshop, and manages the money he earns there. He visits with his family on weekends and has a circle of acquaintances who are like him. They enjoy such activities as bowling, hiking, swimming, and going to the movies in supervised groups. He continues to have his "special interests" that do not relate to his getting along in life, and thinks about them continually.

Anna

Anna was so cute and so bright that no one suspected a problem until she turned four and a half. At that point her parents and grandmother compared notes and realized that:

- almost everything she said was a repetition of what she had heard on the TV, the radio, her record player, or from someone in the family
- she had begun talking "a bit late" (at about 30 months)
- she had very set habits, such as lining up all her dolls by height and her crayons by color several times each day
- she would only wear soft loose-fitting clothes
- she sometimes seemed not to hear and other times covered her ears when certain songs came on the radio
- about age three she had turned from liking to be alone to being very friendly and going to everyone she met, including strangers, with no show of concern.

Anna's grandfather was described as a loner, an odd duck, and antisocial. He had died before Anna was born. Otherwise her family history was unremarkable. Anna had been born at exactly five pounds after a difficult pregnancy, with bleeding reported during the last part of the middle trimester. Her delivery and postnatal health history were quite normal except for several bouts of middle ear infections, which had not been treated with antibiotics.

Anna was first evaluated by a developmental pediatrician who suspected mild autism and referred her to me to make sure. When we met she was just five years old. At the outset of her diagnostic interview she started playing with a teddy bear selected from a toy bin I kept under my desk. She began telling it to be "a good teddy bear or I'll take you to the doctor." Believe it or not, she persisted with this same play theme for the whole hour, talking to the teddy bear as her mother had talked to her, as her father had talked to her, and as her grandmother had talked to her. I could clearly make out her echoing these three different adult voices. A few times I saw her flicking her fingers and rubbing the teddy bear's fur in a rhythmic manner. These behaviors would have escaped notice but for the fact that I was specifically looking for them.

What is your diagnosis? What is your prognosis?

Here are my thoughts:

Anna has typical mild delays and spurts of development, disturbances in relating and language development, and sensory-motor problems, which place her in the diagnostic category of autistic disturbance, mild/high-functioning type.

Children with mild symptoms like Anna before age five have a very favorable prognosis. I recommended that she attend a regular education classroom with special educational support, a shadow teacher, and behavior therapy outside of school. I am so optimistic about her that I believe she may continue to improve to the point where I could reclassify her as having Asperger's disorder. Even more optimistic, she is the type of girl who could become so well adapted to her minimal symptoms as an adult that she could become subclinical and fade from our medical view.

Alex – "The Little Professor"

Alex got his nickname, The Little Professor, when he was only five. It was not meant to be a put down in any way, his mother told me. "No, it's just the best way we found to describe what kind of a kid he was."

Alex's older brother, Alan, had ADD (attention deficit disorder) and was enrolled in one of our research projects at UCLA. When I learned, quite by chance, that his younger brother Alex was called The Little Professor, this sparked my curiosity and I asked his mother to describe him. As she told me about him, I smiled to myself and I thought, "Maybe 'Little Professor' is a new term for Asperger's disorder?"

We contacted Alan's parents and I re-interviewed them with my focus this time on Alex. What I found out was fascinating. Alex's mother gave me the following history:

> There were no problems during Alex's pregnancy or delivery, and he was always healthy. He was a calm and quiet little baby who made no demands, nursed easily, slept well, and always seemed to be happy. He gazed at me OK and he cooed and babbled OK on time. He was a little late sitting up and walking, but by one and a half had caught up. But, he still is clumsy when we compare him to other kids in the neighborhood.

Alex started to talk just before he was two years old. And by three he had taught himself to read by watching *Big Bird* and other educational TV programs over and over again. I didn't even need to encourage this, it came naturally, he just loved to watch them over and over again by himself. By four he could read like a grownup for hours on end. When he was four and a half he learned to play checkers and then switched right away to chess on his own. He would only play with his father, and this was the only game he liked.

We hardly knew he was around the house. He was always quiet, took care of his own clothes and things. When he reached four and a half we sent him to school for the first time. They called him "highly gifted." Since he was clumsy and refused to play any ball-type sports, the other kids always hated him. He never got into rough-and-tumble play with other kids.

Alex never had a pal or even a close friend. His brother and his sister never spent time with him, and he never seemed interest in what they were doing either. He spent all his free time at school or at home reading or collecting and playing with things that happened to interest him. He got a big, big collection of travel brochures, airline schedules, and sports cards. He would collect one thing for weeks or months, then suddenly lose interest and change to collecting something else. He was always teacher's pet because he never caused trouble and always knew the answers to their questions.

But most strange to his mother and father was this:

He seems never to need me, not now or when he was a little baby. He was never one to give hugs or kisses. This is so unlike his sister and even his ADD brother. He never asks how we are feeling, he never tells us how he is feeling inside, and he never wants to join in what we are doing. He never shows sympathy or even gets curious if someone is hurt. It's as if he doesn't need the rest of our family. He knows what's going on with us, but, now that I think about it, it's like he's looking at us from another planet.

When I interviewed our "little professor" he was only eight years old, but I had the feeling I was talking to an 80-year-old British aristocrat. He sat upright in the big chair at the corner of my desk and we conversed as adults.
"Why do you want to talk to me?"
"Yes, I will be glad to answer your questions."
"What kind of a doctor are you?"

"Yes, I like school."

"Yes, I have all the friends I need or wanted."

"Yes, I get along with everyone at home."

"No, I do not like to talk to strangers like you, or anyone."

"Yes, I only like to play alone not with my brother or sister."

"No, I do not know what I want to be when I grow up."

"Yes, I do dream at night, but I never remember what about."

"I already told you, I have all the friends I need."

"No, I will not tell you about them, please do not ask again."

"Are you finished asking me questions? I want to stop talking."

And so it went for the first hour, and then the second hour. He revealed no emotions, no fantasies, no wishes, no frustrations, and no joys. He was like a little reporter sending me a newspaper article describing his life in the most superficial terms.

What is your diagnosis? What is your prognosis?

Here are my thoughts:

My first guess, that our "little professor" had Asperger's disorder, was borne out after reviewing his developmental history, two diagnostic interviews, and talking to his schoolteacher. His parents were not too surprised when they heard my diagnosis, confessing that they had been suspicious that he was socially delayed since he started school.

The keys to his diagnosis were that his major developmental delays were along the pathways of relatedness and language. He started speaking on time, did not have echolalia, but did have typical concrete thinking patterns (he perseverated on special interests which changed frequently, he collected things that had special value only for him, etc.). And most telling, his major developmental delay was his limited capacity to relate to others. He was socially isolated way beyond being just shy, he did not show curiosity about or empathy for others, and preferred to be alone. He never had a friend, never showed a need for one, and even remained socially aloof from his parents and siblings.

With regard to treatment, I recommended that Alex join a weekly social skills training group for kids his age with Asperger's disorder at a local clinic, that he join a chess club and a drama workshop for kids his age, that he begin non-contact martial arts training on an individual basis, that he be encouraged to have "play dates" after school with his cousins and schoolmates, and that his sister and brother set aside time to play with him on a regularly scheduled basis each week.

Alex's prognosis is excellent. His strengths are his obviously high intellectual endowment, his calm temperament (assuming it stays that way through adolescence), and his desire to be liked and to gain the approval of adults (and in the future his peers). His family is most supportive, and this is a crucial factor in his favor. He is the kind of child who can progress through regular secondary schools and do well in college. He can become a completely self-supporting adult (and marry and have children if he so wishes).

Sammy

A pediatrician friend called one Saturday afternoon and asked if I would make time as soon as possible to see a 22-month-old boy who he thought might have autism. He apologized for calling on the weekend, but said the parents were very scared, and he didn't want them to wait a moment longer than necessary for an appointment. "Sure, have them call," I said.

Almost as soon as I put down the phone, it seemed, they called. I cleared out an hour for them the next day and it turned out they were indeed very anxious and scared. Although both were both highly trained professionals, when they heard the word "autism" from their pediatrician it meant that their beautiful little baby boy was "brain damaged, would never speak, was retarded, lost to them for ever."

It turned out that Sammy's family history was unremarkable, as was his medical history, and his mother's pregnancy. He has a healthy older brother who helps care for him. He was a quiet and yet responsive infant who babbled and looked at his parents and others till shortly after his first birthday. Then he gradually became aloof, stopped vocalizing, and by 18 months had stopped gazing at people. He sat up and walked on schedule. He is quite well coordinated and can climb on anything. During my diagnostic interview he did not seem to notice or relate to me at all, not giving me even a glance. He spent the entire hour lining up toy train tracks, spinning the wheels of the toy train while staring at them, running in small circles, jumping repetitively, and turning on and off my light switch. The room remained eerily quiet; he made no sounds at all. He separated from his parents without so much as a look back.

What is your diagnosis? What is your prognosis for this little boy?

Here are my thoughts:

As far as his diagnosis goes, I thought Sammy's pediatrician was correct; he has autistic disorder, severe type. However, I told his parents after our initial diagnostic sessions that I wanted to keep an open mind until he reached 36 months of age. That is the cut-off age for me to be absolutely certain. Given this reservation, however, I recommended that we start treatment right away.

Sammy's parents wasted no time in getting things organized. We began with two hours a day of discrete trial therapy (behavior therapy), and weekly occupational therapy and speech and language therapy. Special education in a classroom for autistic pupils in a public school was added when he turned five.

Sammy is now nine. When he reached four and a half he started to say a few words, which were only used to label things he wanted. He also began at that time to point to pictures of what he wanted. At five and a half he started to echo his parents and the TV set. Over the next two years the echoing decreased and he started to use spontaneous language with some appropriate symbolic usage. He is moderately hyperactive and prone to run off if left alone. Because of this I evaluated him for attention deficit disorder (ADD). After one dose of a very small amount of Ritalin he became even more hyperactive for two hours, thus failing to show the diagnostic "paradoxical response" of slowing down on a stimulant. That was the first and last time we tried that approach. But it was an experiment worth trying because it caused no harm and ruled out a possibly treatable co-occurring disorder.

To this day he remains generally aloof. He hugs and kisses, but in a mechanical manner. He still does not use eye contact consistently. Rather, he will look at you if he needs something, and then only for a few moments. He continues to have repetitive behaviors like spinning, staring at things going around, and flicking light switches on and off, and is sensitive to certain sounds and textures.

With regard to his specific diagnosis, when Sammy's language began and he had developmental spurts in other areas I moved him from the severe to the mild/high-functioning category. As I discussed in earlier chapters I have never seen a child regress from the mild/high-functioning category back to the severe category. This fact, together with the expectation that he can and probably will have further developmental spurts till he reaches his twenties, let me give his parents some reason for cautious optimism.

Mr. C

I had a recent phone conversation that went this way:

> Hello – is this the doctor? – I have been reading about Asperger's disorder on the internet – and found your name on the internet – I want to see if that's what I have – could you do that for me? – I was born in 1947 – I can come in any time that you want.

All that was said in one long run-on sentence, in a staccato rhythm with no inflections. And then he paused for a breath.

Mr. C opened the door to my office within a few milliseconds of our appointment time. His clothes were old and shabby, his hair disheveled, and his shoes scuffed up. After a limp handshake, no eye contact, and no formal greeting he launched into his story:

"I told you on the phone why I wanted to talk to you. I never fitted in. Here is a letter a doctor gave my mother when I as a little boy." (The letter was from his kindergarten teacher. I am going to quote a good deal of it because it is so moving. Remember, it was written in 1952, when his teacher knew nothing of autism, and 30 years before Asperger's disorder was even described in the English language.)

> During this semester he has worked and played alone. Boys push him away, and he will rerun to the activity again and again until they get rough. He almost never expresses himself verbally to other children. His fear of other children has mostly disappeared. He needs to be dealt with on an individual level. He is seeking attention from the other children now but lacks the social skills. When he decides on a job he is persistent about carrying it through despite obstacles or his own lack of skill… He still does more observing of others than participation in activities. For a long while he participated in nothing. He usually requires teacher suggestions to get him engaged in an activity. He never engages in sand or mud play. His ability to coordinate large muscle movement is beginning to improve. He is beginning to catch up physically. He is just beginning to work on the task of learning to interact with the other children. As yet he has not been able to function as a member of a group; it may be too much to expect him to make enough of a start on these tasks to qualify him for first graded work next Fall.

He was referred to his school's psychologist when he was in the first grade. No specific diagnosis was given but he received tutoring on and off for the rest of elementary school and high school. He told me he never "got it" as far as what interested other children. "I stayed by myself all the time and did what I wanted to do." What he wanted to do was read and "do research" about subjects like the French Revolution, Shakespeare, Lord Nelson's sea battles, and the Civil War. This research meant he had to spend many hours in libraries. While in college he majored in library sciences, got As and Bs in all his subjects, and lived alone while being supported by his parents. When I asked him about his social life and dating during college he said, with no hesitation or emotion, "Since I learned to masturbate when I was 15 I did not need to have a girlfriend or a woman in my life."

After college he found a job as a librarian. There he met a woman librarian who, he said, "started our relationship and wanted to marry me." They were married after three years of dating and have been together ever since. When I asked him what married life was like he answered, "We live side by side, she does what she likes and I do what I like." When I asked about his romantic life he said, "We always had a routine sex life, I was never too interested and she wasn't either." He added that they had agreed not to have children before they were married.

Mr. C had a checkered work history. He was fired from several library jobs because, "I couldn't fit in with the people who worked there. I never could see the point of talking to people unless there was a point to it, and that got me fired." After trying several other jobs he landed one as an assistant teacher with developmentally delayed children. He liked this and did it for six years. He said, "I felt very comfortable with the children, I could keep them happy." However, his inability to communicate with his coworkers and supervisors led to his being relocated several times, and eventually fired. He had been unemployed for several months when we met. His wife, who still worked as a librarian, was supporting him.

Mr. C had a checkered medical history too! Following high school his difficulty "reading people" increasingly troubled him. He knew he thought differently from others. Because of these concerns he sought psychiatric consultations on several occasions as the years went by, and had been labeled "schizoid," "bipolar," "borderline," "neurotic," and "depressed." One doctor who thought he had attention deficit disorder tried him on Ritalin. This he said "speeded my brain up so I never did that stuff again." Other doctors had prescribed antidepressants and antipsychotics with equally ineffective results. He had not been on medication for several years when we met.

What is your diagnosis? What is you prognosis?

Here are my thoughts:

Mr. C's life story is right out of the diagnostic book when it comes to describing Asperger's disorder. He had no prenatal or postnatal medical problems and started to talk on time. His kindergarten teacher observed that at age five he had mild gross and fine motor delays, severe delays in the capacity to relate to adults and peers, and a very concrete and perseverative thinking style.

His early developmental delays in language and relatedness plagued him his entire life. Being "socially blind" he has been unable to understand other people, to form deep friendships, or to get along with supervisors well enough to hold a job. He has always had special interests that do not relate to his getting along in life, and thinks about them continually.

His prognosis is that he is not likely to change much as the years roll by. He is fortunate to be married to a woman who accepts him as he is and is content to support him both financially and socially. He has little need for outside emotional contact or support.

Mr. C showed no emotion when I confirmed his suspicions that he had Asperger's disorder. He only said, "I can now stop looking for other explanations for what kind of a person I am." I recommended that he might benefit from joining a support group and talking with other adults who have Asperger's disorder. He simply looked at the floor, and said in a flat monotone, "I'll have to think about it." We left it at that. I doubt whether the future will hold much new for him.

Fred

Although only 19 when we met, Fred had already had three major "breakdowns." The last happened one week after he left home for college in a distant city, just before we met. He had made the long trip alone by car, enrolled in school, and set up a little apartment with no difficulty. Then, a week later, he called home saying he couldn't concentrate, felt depressed, and was "breaking down again."

Fred's first breakdown "hit him" (his words) when he was 14. He locked himself in his room and stopped talking. He was placed in a psychiatric hospital for a month and slowly recovered. The next year, when 15, he had an identical breakdown, recovered in a few weeks, only to have an identical relapse when he was 17.

Fred had been in treatment since his first breakdown at 14 with a psychiatrist whose diagnosis was "major depressive disorder." His doctor had seen him regularly for counseling psychotherapy and had tried him on all the usual antidepressant medications, obviously with no success. He was considering switching him to antipsychotic medication after his last break-down, but wanted a consultation before taking this step to see if something else might be going on. This is how I got into the picture.

During our first interview Fred said little and related in a stiff and stilted manner. He hardly looked at me and was very reluctant to say any-thing but "yes" and "no," even to my most non-directive questions. During our second interview he told me he liked to think "only about special things." When I pursued this he finally opened up and started talking non-stop. He knew "his things" were not what others thought were impor-tant or interesting. They included memorizing facts about old maps, his-toric battles, and famous generals and admirals.

Early in high school he decided he would join the Reserve Officers' Training Corps when he got to college and become a career officer in the army. He learned all he could about this program and military life. This dream crashed into the reality when he realized that he was unable to arrange his own life after leaving home for college. At the conclusion of this interview I asked him to do some "homework" so we could together figure out what was causing his breakdowns. He agreed to write a brief autobiog-raphy before our next session.

During our third interview we went over his homework. He portrayed his early years as very hard, knowing that he didn't like to be with other kids and unable to understand how other people thought and felt about each other. He always preferred to be alone, to be able to think about what he was interested in at the time, and hated to have to worry all the time how to please his parents and teachers. He described how he gave up when he had his breakdowns: "I just stopped trying." This is what he and his psychi-atrist agreed to call "depression." (This is far from what is usually consid-ered depression in medical terms.) He knew all the pills he took only made him sleepy, but did not want to fight his doctor, "so I always took them."

Fred's parents confirmed the fact that he had always been a loner, socially awkward, and a mystery to everyone since he was four or five years old. He had started to speak on time, his motor milestones were passed at the right time, and he had always been in good physical health. There was no autism in his family.

What is your diagnosis and prognosis?

Here are my thoughts:

Fred was misdiagnosed as having a depressive disorder. He certainly got discouraged, and he certainly looked depressed when he had a "breakdown," but he never had morbid or depressed mood changes. Rather, he had found a way to tune out of a world that he couldn't understand and couldn't figure out how to cope with. He withdrew and "gave up for a while," to quote his words. His diagnosis became clear when we reviewed his life course. From his earliest years on he had a major developmental lag in his capacity to relate to others. His symbolic language processing had plateaued, leaving his thinking style concrete and focused on special areas of interest he could master by memorizing. He has a classic case of Asperger's disorder.

Fred's future is quite bright. I reviewed the nature of his problems with his family and we set up a therapy program. First he was to live in an apartment nearby his home. Second, all psychoactive medications would be discontinued. Third, a "social coach" would be found who could help him learn to feel comfortable with himself, and to be able to accept himself just as he is. Fourth, we agreed that no expectations as to returning to school or choosing a career would be placed on him for at least a year, and then only after he had had a chance to figure out such issues with his coach. Taking away pressures that were unrealistic for him was the keystone of his treatment. He needs time to catch up psychologically and emotionally to his chronological age. Finally, he would be helped to find a job that would require minimal contact with coworkers, and be well within his abilities and interests so as to assure success.

I am quite certain that given time, patience, and the right social skills coaching Fred can lead an independent, self-supporting adult life.

Autistic parents of autistic children

This section of the casebook contains brief descriptions of 14 parents who have either autism or Asperger's disorder. Their life stories present the broad range of what adult life can have in store for those with these disorders.

I first wrote about some of these autistic parents in 1994. They were the first ones ever described in the medical literature and I discovered them while working with their autistic children. Since then I have met many more such parents of autistic children (as well as many autistic parents who do not have children with autism or Asperger's disorder).

Parent #1

He was born in 1917, in England, and was the father of one autistic son (born 1952, IQ reported to be 70), one autistic daughter (born 1958, IQ reported to be 45), and five non-autistic children, two sons and three daughters. He had a law degree, but he had been fired from several legal positions because of social ineptitude and inability to understand legal principles. He translated legal documents for more than 20 years from French to English. His spouse's comments were as follows:

> I knew he was odd, a loner, but brilliant; he always needed strict routines. When we met I courted him. Living with him is like living alone. He never had friends or a social life. He has no sexual problems, but his interest is low. He was known to be a shy, odd child who was picked on, but protected by college acquaintances. He was always ritualistic about clothes, and kept the same schedules of eating and dressing year after year. He attends to our children in an aloof manner. He is closest to our autistic son with whom he lived when our son was a teenager and he and I were separated. He is perfectly multilingual but very literal.

At the time of the mental status exam he was tall and gaunt. He had an awkward gait, but good coordination. His affect was shallow and unchanging, with a vacuous smile maintained throughout the interview. He appeared socially awkward, had no sense of humor, was eager to please, and was well oriented. He stared off into space while conversing in a monotone. He attended to his son in a mechanical, stilted way and showed no curiosity about my visit or the venipuncture I did for research. He was uninterested in his wife or children's whereabouts or their health.

Parent #2

He was born in 1937, in Utah, and is the father of five autistic children (daughter born 1957, IQ reported to be 25; son born 1964, IQ reported to be 23; son born 1966, IQ reported to be 27; daughter born 1968, IQ reported to be 25; son born 1971, deceased 1987, IQ reported to be 35) and one non-autistic son. He had a high school education and one year of trade school. He was a clerk in a tool room for a railroad, working the midnight to 8 AM shift for more than 15 years. His income was always marginal, and he periodically required welfare assistance. His spouse was uncooperative, disheveled, and withdrawn, and was reported by a welfare worker to be borderline mentally retarded and depressed. At the time of the mental status examination he was disheveled and obese, maintained a constant vacuous smile, had a flat affect, was socially inappropriate, had no sense of humor, but had an excellent rote memory. He spoke to his autistic children in Dutch and English. He knew three other languages and was learning Russian "just because I like languages." He was completely unaware of the social implications of his children's disabilities. He was falsely accused of child molestation and was not even aware of the meaning or consequences of this. He attended only to concrete issues.

Parent #3

This parent was born in 1926, in Idaho. He was the father of one autistic son (born 1957, IQ reported to be 67), one autistic daughter (born 1973, IQ reported to be 74), one non-autistic daughter, and two non-autistic sons. He had a high school education, but he was fired from many jobs due to perseverative conversations about religion, pipe organs, etc. His spouse commented:

> He was always a loner, socially awkward, and inappropriate from early school years. He never held a job for long, as he talked about his special interests to everyone all the time. He memorized three bibles, organ stops for numerous organs throughout the country, and hundreds of useless historical facts. He always had rituals and elaborate routines, and never understood other people's feelings. He hand-flapped and lined up objects throughout all of his adult life. Regarding sex, he learned what he had to do and did it. He had a low sex drive, but no unusual behaviors or interests. He has definite autism. Our marriage was arranged by our families. He's kindly but distant from our children.

At the time of the mental status examination he was obese and clean, but had an old style of dress. He kept a cheerful attitude throughout, even when discussing problems. He believed he had autism like his two children. He hand-flapped and perseverated on non-relevant information when not directed. He was aware of being unable to tell about others' feelings. He died in 1989 of an apparent heart attack.

Parent #4

This parent was born in 1945, in Massachusetts, and was the father of one autistic son (born 1984, IQ reported to be 87) and one non-autistic son. He had a Ph.D. in Arts and Letters. His spouse commented:

He was fat and awkward, always picked on and isolated when young. Now he only has professional acquaintances. He got A grades in classes that fitted his preoccupations, but did poorly in math and chemistry. He has an excellent rote memory, is multilingual (eight languages), but has little empathy and is not sensitive to others' feelings. He tunes out. He never does anything part way. He is obsessive and has some mannerisms. He has many characteristics of our autistic son. I am convinced he has autism. He speaks Latin at home.

At the time of the mental status examination, his appearance and dress were normal. He gave very direct and specific answers. He showed no insight, but said that he understood his autistic son and believed they shared some characteristics. He denied any need for friends and relied on his wife to run the household, pay bills, etc. His affect was unvarying while discussing problems, and his thoughts were very concrete.

Parent #5

He was born in 1934, in Oregon, and is the father of one autistic son (born 1973, IQ reported to be 20), one autistic daughter (born 1972, IQ reported to be 21), and one non-autistic daughter. He had a Bachelor of Arts degree and one year of graduate accounting, but had lost several accounting jobs because he could not handle complex concepts, schedule changes, or form professional relationships. He worked as a mold polisher for 23 years at the same factory. His spouse commented:

> I knew he was odd from the start. Now I'm convinced he has autism just like the children, no doubt about it. He's been socially inept since childhood, and was labeled retarded until age nine years when baby talk ended and he began school. He had failing grades until the fourth grade, and then he got As and Bs. He never had a friend. We met at a church social; I initiated and pursued the relationship. He never showed empathy. He had hand-flapped and bit himself throughout adulthood. He shows decreased response to pain. He walks in the woods by himself as his only relaxation. He knows everything about knives, guns, and his garden, which he visits several times a day. Sex was mechanical and initiated by me. We have had no sexual relations for the past 10 years.

At the time of the mental status examination, he was disheveled and awkward, and had stilted mannerisms. He had an atonal voice and flat affect. He perseverated on his interests unless redirected. He paced and hand-flapped intermittently, repeated words and phrases, and was unable to discuss his family or his three children's problems. He had no insight.

Parent #6

This parent was born in 1957, in Massachusetts, and is the father of an autistic son. He had a Bachelor of Arts degree and had taken Masters level courses in electrical engineering, but he could not "get things together to complete my degree." He performed reliability checks on electronic equipment. His spouse reported:

> According to his mother, he had delayed onset of speech, echolalia, peculiar mannerisms, and preoccupation with spinning objects and soft textures. He was socially isolated when a child, which led to psychiatric treatment from age four to seven. He was always bullied and aloof in school and never had a friend. He did well by memorizing. He has always been clumsy, uncoordinated, and had a poor gait since childhood. We met at a singles party, and I knew at first sight that I should marry him. I take care of him, as he is socially withdrawn and preoccupied with his special interests in computers and engineering. Math is his best subject. He always likes to stare at spinning things and watch television with our autistic child. We have been convinced for years that he has autism.

At the time of the mental status examination, he was appropriately dressed, socially awkward, obviously uncomfortable, and he talked in a monotone about his habits, rituals, and peculiar interests. He related that he had measured the frequencies that make him feel calm when he stares at a strobe light. He was concerned but not empathetic about his son, maintained a constant shallow inappropriate smile, and had an unchanging affect throughout the interview. He believed he shared some of his son's problems, but had no insight into these problems or into his own personality. He acknowledged his dependency on his wife to manage their social and family life. He denied having sexual problems, but stated that sex did not interest him.

Parent #7

This parent was born in 1947, in California, and is the father of two autistic sons (born 1976, IQ reported to be 113; born 1981, IQ reported to be 70). He had a Bachelor of Arts degree and five years of graduate engineering, but he did not write the thesis needed to obtain his Ph.D. He was a computer programmer. His spouse commented:

> His parents told me that as a child he was always a loner, had mannerisms, and always spoke in a long, boring way. He never socially tuned in, and needed routines. He has no imagination, did well in math, can play and read music, but cannot write it. He never had empathy and cannot complete tasks at home or at work because he becomes preoccupied with details. He shows no creativity in his programming work. He was always clumsy and not interested in sports or physical activity. I manage all the family affairs and tell him what to do. Our sex life is non-existent.

At the time of the mental status examination he was appropriately dressed, socially awkward, spoke in long, atonal pedantic phrases, and showed no empathy or understanding of his children's problems. He knows that he is like them and believes that he has autism. He denies sexual problems. He walked on his toes, paced, hummed constantly, hand-flapped, and repeated phrases.

Parent #8

This woman was born in 1952, in California, and is the wife of Parent #7. She had a Bachelor of Arts degree and one year of laboratory technician school. She was a laboratory technologist in a toxicology laboratory. Her spouse's comments were not available, but her self-description was as follows:

> I have autism, my husband does, too. I'm more like my older son; my husband is more like my younger son. When young, I knew I was odd and socially different. I was taken to various psychologists during childhood, but never given a diagnosis. They all concluded the same – I'm brilliant but odd. I was bullied at school and had no friends. I had an excellent memory; I memorized all of "Goldilocks" when I was only three years old. I got As in school. I even joined Mensa, and my IQ is over 150. I was socially out of tune and withdrawn, but got better after my teen years. I still tune out, hand-flap, jump on a trampoline for two to three hours per day, body-rock, and toe-walk. However, I don't need to spin anymore. I share social-relating, motor, and sensory symptoms with both my sons. I knew my husband was odd from the start, and I take care of him. I feel my high IQ has saved me.

At the mental status examination, she was appropriately dressed, very talkative, and knowledgeable about autism and symptoms in herself, in her two sons, and her husband. Her affect was unchanging, and she denied having any sexual problems.

Parent #9

He was born in 1944, in Utah, and is the father of one autistic son (born 1972, IQ reported to be 68). He was divorced and remarried. He had a high school diploma and four years of trade school. He had spray-painted fenders of cars for more than 20 years. His spouse commented:

> I knew he was peculiar and had to be taken care of when we married. I was told he was very shy and quiet as a child and had no friends, and he remains socially isolated as an adult. After painting cars all day, he goes down to his basement workshop and paints miniature trains. He is never involved with his son or our family life. We have no sexual problems, but his urge is low. He is very withdrawn and nonsocial; he is a serious concern, like an autistic himself.

At the mental status examination, he was shabbily dressed, socially awkward, and uncomfortable. His affect was shallow and unchanging. He was aware that he was different, needing routines and not wanting to have friends. He said, "I think about my work. I'm introverted. My wife is the social one. I avoid the family." He acknowledged tuning out others and not having feelings for others.

Parent #10

This patient was born in 1935, in Utah, and is the father of two autistic sons (born 1973, IQ reported to be 101; born 1981, IQ reported to be 66) and three non-autistic children, two daughters and one son. He had a Masters degree in library science, and his job entailed cataloguing books in a library. His spouse commented:

> He walked at 24 months, was isolated and bullied in grade school. He was called petunia head, and he thought it was a favorable sign of attention. He has hand-flapped, snapped his fingers, and stared at wheels of toy trains throughout his adulthood. He is clumsy and uncoordinated, so he never played sports. He had no friends in school or college. He has perfect recall for maps and numbers, keeps population figures in his head, and composes perseverative music. His interest in sex is minimal. It took him a long time to learn what to

do, and he is mechanical. He is distant and insensitive to his children, and he lacks empathy. He cannot handle any changes in his daily routines. I knew he was different, but I was 29 and felt he was "my best chance" because he was stable. I take care of him. He speaks four languages and reads and writes three others. He spends most of his time at home making elaborate, miniature amusement parks with multilingual signs.

At the mental status examination, he was appropriately dressed and socially uncomfortable, and he gave concrete, lengthy, and pedantic answers. He perseverated on his interests. His affect was flat and unchanging. He showed no insight or empathy for his children.

Parent #11

This patient was born in 1949, in Utah, and is the father of one autistic daughter (born 1982, IQ reported to be 55) and five non-autistic children, two daughters and three sons. He had Associate of Arts degrees in electronics and accounting. He had intermittently worked as a computer technician for 10 years, but recently was fired because he "rocked all the time." He tried to work as a salesman. His spouse commented:

> He's been known to body-rock hours per day since childhood and repeated fourth grade three times due to daydreaming. He's in his own world, has no friends, is not good at sports, and always needs routines. He proposed immediately after we met even though I didn't even know his name. He compulsively masturbated through adolescence and young adulthood, and learned to have mechanical intercourse because he told me he wanted to do it just right. I manage our household, plan everything in advance and have to tell him, even if I go out for an hour, or otherwise he falls apart. He never had any friends. He can play any musical instrument, is skilled with computers, speaks English and French, and memorizes religious information. All his clothes must coordinate, and he has to dress in a certain order.

At the mental status examination, he was appropriately dressed, stilted in manner, very concrete, and stated that he has a mild form of autism. He said, "When I was small they thought I was autistic. I never had friends. I had difficulty putting my thoughts into words. I couldn't do math." During the interview he stared blankly and body-rocked. His affect was pleasant but unchanging, and he gave lengthy answers about his particular interests.

Parent #12

This woman was born in 1947, in Utah, and is the mother of one autistic son (born 1968, IQ reported to be 83), three autistic daughters (born 1970, IQ reported to be 105; born 1976, IQ reported to be 36; born 1978, IQ reported to be 89), and one non-autistic daughter. Her education consisted of high school plus one year of community college. She performed occasional unskilled work, was usually on welfare, and needed others to care for her children. Her husband was thought to have committed suicide by a drug overdose. She said of herself that she was obsessive and unable to manage her household, money, and child-rearing responsibilities. She had always had a good rote memory, but said she could not read gestures or other people's faces and had always spoken in a long rambling manner. She said she had many habits, such as rubbing velvet. She never had a friend or social life. She became preoccupied with useless information, such as repetitively reading genealogy records instead of attending to her children, cleaning, or cooking. At the mental status examination, she was disheveled and dirty. Her house was unkempt, with unsupervised children running with no shoes on among broken glass while she read genealogy records and answered questions. She was interviewed another time at a bus stop and diner because she had gotten preoccupied with putting on makeup on the way to the clinic and called to ask us if we could meet her. She gave lengthy answers and perseverated on her interests. She was loud and socially inappropriate. She did not know the whereabouts of, or show any concern for, her non-autistic daughter, who was in placement in a foster home.

Parent #13

This man was born in 1929, in Utah, and is the father of two autistic sons (born 1961, IQ reported to be 137; born 1970, IQ reported to be 80) and five non-autistic children. He could not graduate from high school, despite an IQ of 121, due to perseverating and social ineptitude. He intermittently worked as a salesman and dance teacher, but was usually on welfare. His spouse commented:

> He has the same problems as our two autistic sons; he repeats activities and phrases, speaks in monologues – like lecturing. He wrote and practiced compulsively his sales talks, which he delivered by rote, since he has no spontaneous conversation skills. He had been socially isolated since childhood, is unable to relate, copies and echoes feelings, and was always bullied in school, where he could not do well despite

his high IQ. He is oblivious to his social and work problems. He has a normal sex drive, but performs with no feelings. He uses me as an object.

At the mental status examination, he was appropriately dressed and socially awkward, had an atonal voice and limited conversation, paced the room, gave only concrete answers, and had no insight, and his affect was flat and unchanging.

Parent #14

This woman was born in 1940, in Utah, and is the mother of one autistic son (born 1968, IQ reported to be 91) and two non-autistic half-siblings. In her self-report she stated:

> I was never told I was late talking or developing physically. I sat with girls in school, and they smiled at me. We didn't do anything together – did that make us friends? I borrowed a smile from my imaginary friend. Never to this day do I understand what people are about. I thought going to Vietnam was going on vacation. I learned to read mechanically. I have to read a story or book by learning person, place, and thing. I learn only by pictures. My sister told me I can't process information and give it the same meaning other people do. A psychology instructor in 1988 said I had autism because my tests showed I know all details but I can't connect information and make sense of it. I like to think about my breathing. I like to spin around and go backwards. I like to feel and bite smooth things (e.g., egg shells). When I was young I flapped my hands, was fascinated by staring at lights, was sensitive to sounds, pain, and cold, sometimes not. I still like to stare at fans. I never dated, but went to school with a man who chose me. I was scared to say no to marriage. We had no real sex life. He divorced me, said I was strange. Then I met my autistic son's father. He chose me, but I have not married him because I am afraid he'd find out I'm strange. I found out with him why other people like sex. I graduated high school, but I never worked; I was always on welfare. I never had friends or socialized. I am now going to school. I need to arrive two hours early to be sure I can sit at the same desk. If not, I get lost, disoriented, and have to go home. I need tutors for every subject. They use pictures to help me. My (autistic) son and I are so much alike, we're not so grounded. We don't process like other people. He has autism. I know I have what he has (do you have autism?). But I don't know if I have autism. I think my sister's son has autism. He can't learn what things mean.

At the time of the mental status examination, she was well groomed, obviously socially awkward, and uncomfortable. She gave lengthy, concrete, and perseverative answers. She was tearful and fearful until reassured that she was being cooperative. She had no insight into the nature of autism, but was aware of her symptoms and social problems. She appeared of average intelligence, but had restricted interests and a narrow range of information.

Chapter 8

The Importance
of Obtaining
a Diagnosis

On diagnosis

Sadly, often I hear people saying that getting a diagnosis is "a waste of time and money." They rationalize by saying it only "pigeon holes" a child, "pins on a useless label," or causes "prejudice."

Whenever I am asked, "Is it important to get a proper diagnosis?" my answer is always, "Absolutely!!" (Could I be more emphatic?) "Diagnose before you treat!" is an old medical school saying which my professors dinned into my head, and which I din into the head of every one of my medical students. It is especially relevant to autism and Asperger's disorder today.

It is true, however, that it was difficult to obtain a proper diagnosis until the 1980s because we doctors had not yet agreed upon diagnostic criteria. In order to solve this problem I put together a committee to formulate objective diagnostic criteria in 1978, when I was the chairman of the Professional Advisory Board of the Autism Society of America. Autism was just "coming out of the closet" as far as the public was concerned. Parents needed ways to obtain services and insurance coverage, and researchers around the world needed a way to make sure they were studying the same patients. I had child psychiatrists, neurologists, psychologists, pediatricians, teachers, occupational therapists, speech and language therapists, and yes, even parents on my committee. We came up with a clinically and developmentally based descriptive definition. We called it, "The National Society for Autistic Children's Definition of Autism," and it was widely published.

Shortly thereafter the medical community began putting together the third edition of the *Diagnostic and Statistical Manual of Mental Disorders*, which became the bible for formal diagnoses. A "Chinese menu" approach was proposed for this definition. (You need so many symptoms from column one, and so many from column two, and the fortune cookie is free). Despite objections from myself and others on the committee (we wanted a developmental approach), the American Psychiatric Association adopted this type of diagnostic system. Since it is the "Gold Standard," accepted by schools, insurance companies, and the medical community, I have reprinted the most recent revision in this book (see chapter 9).

Returning to the question at the beginning of this section: it is crucial not only to get a proper diagnosis, but to get it as soon as possible for two main reasons. First, as I said, proper treatment depends on proper diagnosis. (And the sooner that starts, the better.) Second, parents need an "official" diagnosis by a credentialed professional in order to get services paid for by insurance companies, school districts, and other third-party providers.

For those with mild autism and Asperger's disorder who were not diagnosed during childhood, it is just as vital to obtain an accurate diagnosis when they are older. This is true even if it has been years after the onset of symptoms. Every such person I have diagnosed in their later years has told me that it really helped to be able at last to put a label on their problems. To finally learn that they have a physical disorder which interferes with their ability to think like others and relate to others, and which can cause unusual sensory experiences, and to learn that thousands of others around the world have the same disorder, can be a source of consolation, if not comfort.

In our efforts to educate a new generation of professionals and the public the pendulum may have swung a bit too far. By this I mean that recently I have seen evidence of "overdiagnosis" of cases, especially of Asperger's disorder. For example, of the last ten adults who consulted me to determine if they had Asperger's disorder, eight had "diagnosed" themselves after reading about it on the internet, and two had been "diagnosed" by their spouse. Guess what, eight of the ten were wrong, they did not have it. Thus, their overall batting average was only two hundred in baseball terms, or 20 percent in poker terms. This is what I mean by "overdiagnosis."

How do I make a diagnosis?

To get the complete answer to this question I suggest you enroll in my post-doctoral program at UCLA and give me a year or two of your time. But here I can at least give you an outline of the essential steps I take with children and adults who seek my advice.

I want to give you this outline so you will have an idea of what to expect if and when you are in the position of seeking a diagnosis. It is a highly complex procedure, and it requires much time, thought, and expertise.

Often the diagnostic process gets short-circuited. Sadly, day after day I hear stories like this from frustrated parents who are seeking a second opinion: "I called the 'Very Famous Clinic' and someone there told me after a few minutes on the phone that Freddie definitely has autism."

And just as often I hear from parents that after a half hour visit to a clinic they were told something like this: "Suzie definitely does not have autism."

How these "gurus" can come to such momentous life-altering decisions in such a short time used to puzzle me. But now it is clear. I figured it out after much thought and several long consultations with scientific colleagues around the world. These diagnostic wizards base their opinions on "pure ignorance."

Here are the steps I take when diagnosing severe, and mild/high-functioning autism. It is the process I preach to my students and always practice.

1. I begin by carefully explaining that diagnosis rests on a careful review of the child's medical history and life course, and should be done by someone who has had a lot of experience in this area. At this point I invite questions about my own training and experience. I preface this by pointing out that before I took one of my seven kids to a doctor I made sure that the doctor was an expert in the area of my concern, or I asked right out if I didn't know. Experienced physicians do not take offense at such questions, and if they do, well you have your answer, and go elsewhere. I say this because diagnosing and treating developmental disorders is a team effort. And if you don't feel 100 percent comfortable with your doctor from the start, trouble probably lies ahead for your team, and your child could well be the one who pays the price.

2. Next I explain that there are no special medical or psychological tests that can help us make the diagnosis. There is no X-ray, brain scan, or marker in the blood to help us. Despite years of searching

none has yet been found. Also, there is no single symptom or behavior that alone makes the diagnosis. For example, all normal babies occasionally flap, twirl, have unusual reactions to sound, can be late talkers, echo things, be very shy, and even be unresponsive to others at times.

A medical doctor must always be consulted some time during the diagnostic process since there is always the possibility that some disease besides autism could be present (a child psychiatrist, child neurologist, pediatrician, developmental pediatrician, or family practitioner trained in this area).

3.   Next I review the family history, especially looking for relatives with autism or Asperger's disorder. These are the only disorders that load the dice for autism. Many other conditions such as attention deficit disorder, depression, bipolar disorder, a variety of psychoses and neuroses, Down's syndrome, and other genetic abnormalities have been suggested at one time or another to be more common in families with autism. The fact of the matter is that further research has shown that autism and Asperger's disorder are the only ones that load the dice, genetically speaking.

4.   I then begin zeroing in on the specific diagnosis by asking parents when their "heart," not their head, first sent out a signal that there might be something wrong with their child. With older kids and adults I ask when they first realized that they thought or felt they were different from others, or if and when this was first pointed out to them. This information is crucial as it indicates when developmental arrests and plateaus first appeared.

5.   Now we come to the heart of the diagnostic process, the part that requires experience, and the part that is more art than science. It is the detailed, step-by-step, review of the life course of the three developmental pathways: sensory-motor, language, and relatedness. I keep a clear picture in my mind of the normal milestones along these pathways. I try to pinpoint plateaus and spurts of development, and note separation of the pathways. I ask about specific behaviors and symptoms as I go along each pathway. When this information is not available from a teenager or adult, I ask them to find someone who knew them when they were young and ask for some help.

6.   At the outset of my mental status examination with very little
     children and non-verbal older ones, I explain to the parents that all
     I want to do is spend some time with their child in as natural a
     setting as possible, and get a feel for what he or she is like. We can
     meet at my office, a park, or at their home. It doesn't matter so
     long as their child is comfortable and behaves as usual. No special
     tasks are required as there are with formal educational or
     psychological testing. And parents, siblings, grandparents, and
     nannies can be present if that will help the child to feel more
     comfortable. (Spending time with a crying unhappy child yields no
     useful information.) Once we get started I ask everyone present to
     turn themselves into "furniture," and let me play with their child on
     my own. At first I let the child do what he wants, and only stop
     him if he does something that might be harmful to himself or his
     surroundings. With my being "non-directive," the child can show
     me his true interests. After a while I get more active and join the
     child in whatever he is doing. If he wants to play with some toys
     his parents brought (I ask them to bring his favorite ones) or with
     some of mine, that's OK. If he wants to read, to do repetitive
     things, or nothing at all, that's OK too. At some point I will want
     to hear the tone of his voice, and if he hasn't talked I'll ask a
     parent to try to get some words spoken.

     In my mind I go down a list of things to observe. First I look
for signs of physical illnesses, genetic abnormalities (called
dimorphic features), coordination problems, and other clues of
medical or neurological disorders. When a child is active, agile, and
has age-appropriate gross and fine motor coordination (and no
history of head trauma or seizures) I can be pretty sure his nervous
system is intact. If I see anything unusual I know a neurological
evaluation is in order.

     Next I look carefully for sensory-motor behaviors such as hand
flapping, twirling objects, rubbing surfaces, staring, repetitive
jumping, lining up toys or other objects, turning lights on and off,
spinning things, and all the others described before.

     Then I listen carefully to any word the child volunteers, always
waiting for the child to say things first. This is hard to do (and to
teach) because it is our natural impulse to ask questions and start
conversations with little children. But a child's spontaneous words,
phrases, and ideas are needed to determine his level of language
development. I am asking myself, "Is he mute, in the echo/concrete

phase, or plateaued with difficulty in symbolic processing?" Waiting for 15 minutes in silence for a child to say something can be very frustrating for even the most patient! But learning that a child can remain silent that long and then repeat something he heard on a TV show a week ago could be most useful.

Finally, I look carefully to see how he relates to me, a stranger. Does he ignore me, use me as an object (take my hand and put it on the door knob), crawl onto my lap with no anxiety, cling to his mother, look at me in the eye, get me to play with him, or just play by himself? Again, these questions can only be answered by being very non-directive, simply observing the child without initiation, interaction or asking questions.

Once I have an idea of the child's developmental levels I then change gears and actively engage him in activities that are appropriate to his level of development. If he can read, write, or draw pictures, I try to get him to do these things, if he likes to play video games we do that, if he wants to go exploring my office or the neighborhood, off we go. During this phase of the interview I will also ask his parents to help him to do things, to "show off" a bit. In short I try to find his areas of strength.

Before ending the interview I always ask if I have seen him as he "usually is at home." If he has been cranky, extra shy, or hyperactive because of the unnaturalness of the interview situation, we schedule another session. If everyone feels he has given me a good picture of what his strengths and weaknesses are, then the clinical interview is over.

7.   At this point I figure out if any special psychological or medical testing could help. If so I explain what it is, how we do it, and what it might tell us. There always has to be a very good reason to put a little child in a testing situation, and I only do it if the potential gains are worth it.

8.   After having gathered all the facts I reach for the bible (currently the American Psychiatric Association's *Diagnostic and Statistical Manual of Mental Disorders*, 4th Edition, Text Revision; see chapter 9) and pick out the diagnostic code that best fits my patient. I also note on my records if the patient has primary or secondary autism.

If it is secondary, I make sure that the diagnosis of the underlying cause is made clear to the family or individual, and recommend the appropriate treatment if one is available.

9. I always conclude that a patient has autism, does not have autism, or I am not sure. I never use confusing terms such as "autistic-like," "with autistic features," or "partially autistic." If the diagnosis is not clear I say the three most difficult words in the English language, "I don't know." This usually happens when a child is less than three years old and it's just too early to tell. I recall several infants and toddlers who had been diagnosed as having autism and were brought to me for a second opinion. When I saw them they did not have autism. Did they outgrow it? Probably not. The fact is that they had been too young when first seen, and the person making the diagnosis jumped the gun. Subsequent development by the time they got to me proved they were back on the normal track of development.

10. When the diagnosis is autism or Asperger's disorder I go to great lengths to explain how I arrived at my diagnosis and what it means. This may take several hours, as I have to cover most of the information in this book. If questions remain after my explanation I always leave time to answer them as best as I can. A few minutes at this point can save hours of time later if things remain unclear.

11. After I am sure that the parents have no more questions about how I made the diagnosis and what is wrong, then and only then do we move on to talk about treatment and what the future might hold. I usually use an analogy comparing treatment to sailing. We go over what treatments are indicated, decide which tack to start off on, and when to reevaluate our progress and see if a new tack is indicated.

The clinical interview with mild/high-functioning autistic and Asperger's patients six years or older consists simply of sitting down and talking. Issues of confidentiality and feedback are explained in an age-appropriate manner. The rest of the diagnostic process is much the same as with young children as I described before.

How early and how late can I make a diagnosis?

The answer to the second part of this question is a lot easier, so I'll tackle it first. "It is *never* too late!" (Said in a firm unequivocal tone.)

"Never," if my memory serves me right, refers to a 66-year-old gentleman from Salt Lake City. He is the oldest person with subclinical (previously undiagnosed) Asperger's disorder I have seen to date in my brief career. Fortunately, I was able to document his classic history of unusual perseverative interests and "social blindness" all the way back to his early childhood by interviewing his extended family.

The question of how early I can make a diagnosis is much more complicated. First, infants simply have to have lived long enough and have traveled down the road of life far enough so that you can be certain they have missed crucial normal developmental milestones. Because of this simple fact I never make a firm diagnosis before three years of age. As I just told you, I have seen many infants who were diagnosed with autism before that age who were simply developing slowly. They proved not to have autism at all, rather they were just "developmental slow pokes."

Yes, I certainly can be very suspicious of autism well before the third birthday. And I usually tell this to parents if it is indicated. If my index of suspicion is high enough I may even recommend starting treatment before that age. But I would do this only after explaining my reservations, and that I could be proven wrong by the test of time (and I pray that I am wrong every time I have to go this route).

Chapter 9

The "Official Diagnostic Criteria"

As Shakespeare said, "A rose by any other name would smell as sweet." And so it is with autism. It is what it is, in spite of having had so many names during its brief lifetime. In this section you will find the most recent version of the "official diagnostic criteria." They were published in the *Diagnostic and Statistical Manual of Mental Disorders*, 4th Edition (DSM-IV) of the American Psychiatric Association, in 2000. I served on the committee that wrote these criteria and I assure you it was hard work. Many compromises were made. Since there are no objective tests or physical signs to help us we had to tread across a soft sandy landscape called "clinical judgment." The DSM is a "continuing work in progress," and if you have to work with it professionally and feel frustrated by its limitations, you are in good company, even with those of us who wrote it.

Here are some of the old diagnostic labels that are still in use around the world today. I list them because, strange as it may seem, many patients still carry these old diagnoses, and they are still used in many clinics throughout the world:

- autistic disturbances of affective contact
- idiot savant
- atypical ego development
- atypical autistic disorder
- childhood schizophrenia
- primary autism
- non-organic autism
- mental retardation with autistic features
- autistic-like disorder
- childhood psychosis.

The phrases "autism spectrum disorder" and PDD-NOS (Pervasive Developmental Disorder – Not Otherwise Specified) are also frequently used. They were coined to show the relationship among what we now call severe autism, mild/high-functioning autism, and Asperger's disorder.

Hopefully, we will soon discover clear-cut physical or biological markers of delayed brain development or causative factors, so we can substitute objective measures for clinical judgment when making a diagnosis.

In order to understand these criteria better it may help if you think of a specific child or adult and wonder if he or she "fits." Please remember, no one person has all the criteria, no one criterion is proof of the diagnosis, and the absence of any criteria does not exclude the diagnosis.

As I have stressed elsewhere in this book, the diagnosis rests on identifying separation of developmental pathways, and delays, plateaus, and spurts of development in certain areas of the brain. Only by understanding the normal course of development of these pathways, can you figure out if normal milestones have been missed. This is where "hard science" ends and "the art of diagnosis" begins. Here, then, are the DSM-IV criteria for autistic disorder and Asperger's disorder, with my added comments in square brackets.

Diagnostic criteria for autistic disorder

[As you can see, all the criteria are grouped under three main headings, corresponding to the three main developmental pathways: sensory-motor, language, and relatedness.]

A. A total of six (or more) items from 1, 2, and 3, with at least two from 1 and one each from 2 and 3.

1.   qualitative impairment in social interaction, as manifested by at least two of the following [delays in the relatedness pathway]:

    (a) marked impairment in the use of multiple nonverbal behaviors such as eye-to-eye gaze, facial expression, body postures, and gestures to regulate social interaction

    (b) failure to develop peer relationships, appropriate to developmental level

    (c) a lack of spontaneous seeking to share enjoyment, interests, or achievements with other people (e.g., by a lack of showing, bringing, or pointing out objects of interest)

    (d) lack of social or emotional reciprocity

2.   qualitative impairments in communication as manifested by at least one of the following [delays in the language/cognition pathway]:

(a) delay in, or total lack of, the development of spoken language (not accompanied by an attempt to compensate through alternative modes such as gesture or mime)

(b) in individuals with adequate speech, marked impairment in the ability to initiate or sustain a conversation with others

(c) stereotyped and repetitive use of language or idiosyncratic language

(d) lack of varied, spontaneous make-believe play or social imitative play appropriate to developmental level

3.   restricted, repetitive, and stereotyped patterns of behavior, interests, and activities, as manifested by at least one of the following [delays in the sensory-motor pathway]:

(a) encompassing preoccupation with one or more stereotyped and restricted patterns of interest that is abnormal either in intensity or focus

(b) apparently inflexible adherence to specific, non-functional routines or rituals

(c) stereotyped and repetitive motor mannerisms [e.g., hand or finger flapping or twisting, or complex whole-body movements]

(d) persistent preoccupation with parts of objects

B. Delays or abnormal functioning in at least one of the following areas, with onset prior to age 3 years: (1) social interaction, (2) language as used in social communication, or (3) symbolic or imaginative play. [You should usually reserve final diagnosis until at least 30 to 36 months of age, lest you be fooled.]

C. The disturbance is not better accounted for by Rett's disorder or childhood disintegrative disorder. [And be sure there is no other disease that affects the brain and produces the clinical picture, i.e. secondary autism.]

Diagnostic criteria for Asperger's disorder

A. Qualitative impairment in social interaction, as manifested by at least two of the following [these are also delays in the three pathways, but very mild in the sensory pathway compared to the language and relatedness pathway]:

1.   marked impairment in the use of multiple behaviors such as eye-to-eye gaze, facial expression, body postures, and gestures to regulate social interaction

2.   failure to develop peer relations appropriate to developmental level

3.   a lack of spontaneous seeking to share enjoyment, interests, or achievements with other people [e.g., by a lack of showing, bringing, or pointing out objects of interest to other people]

4.   lack of social or emotional reciprocity

B. Restricted, repetitive, and stereotyped patterns of behavior, interests, and activities, as manifested by at least one of the following [delays in the language/cognitive pathway, especially with attaching proper symbolic meaning]:

1.   encompassing preoccupation with one or more stereotyped and restricted patterns of interest that is abnormal either in intensity or focus

2.   apparently inflexible adherence to specific, nonfunctional routines or rituals

3.   stereotyped and repetitive motor mannerisms (e.g., hand or finger flapping or twisting, or complex whole-body movements) [delay in the sensory-motor pathway]

4.   persistent preoccupation with parts of objects

C. The disturbance causes significant impairment in social, occupational, or other important areas of functioning.

D. There is no clinically significant general delay in language (e.g., single words used by age 2 years, communicative phrases used by age 3 years).

E. There is no significant delay in cognitive development or in the development of age-appropriate self-help skills, adaptive behavior (other than in
social interaction), and curiosity about the environment in childhood.

F. Criteria are not met for another specific pervasive developmental disorder or schizophrenia. [Also be sure to rule out schizoaffective disorder and
social anxiety disorder.]

Epilogue

As sure as the sun rises in the east and sets in the west, someone asks me each time I give a lecture, "How did you pick autism to study in the first place?" and "How on earth did you stick to working on the same disease for over 40 years?" I figure some of you, after reading this far, will want to ask me the same questions, so here are the answers for those of you who do.

Each time I hear the first question, about how I chose to study autism, a vivid image floods my mind. Remember how I told you that some people with mild autism and Asperger's disorder think mainly in vivid pictures? Well, if they do it "wholesale," and the rest of us do it "retail," then this question triggers one of those "retail" moments for me.

The picture I see is of my father, sitting at his old fold-down desk in our den at home. Yellow legal pads filled with his scratchy handwriting are strewn around the room amidst a myriad of old X-ray films. Cigar smell is in the air. He is explaining to me that he has just started to write a series of textbooks on X-ray diagnosis.

I ask him, "Dad, what part of the body are you going to write about in your first book?"

"It will be about X-ray diagnosis of the head," he says softly without looking up.

"But that's the hardest part of the body to study with X-rays, far and away the most difficult part to diagnose. Why did you choose that one?" I blurt out.

He turns his head slowly, looks up at me with a soft knowing look in his gray eyes, and gently but firmly says, "That's exactly why."

Several years later I met my first young patient with autism. He taught me what my father had meant, why he obviously had chosen the head for his first book. I have never forgotten this little boy, even after all these years. His name was Harold.

I was a junior in medical school when Harold's case was presented at a "grand rounds" conference. Harold baffled my professors as much as he baffled me. My psychiatry professor said he had been traumatized by his mother's unconscious hostility. She prescribed psychoanalysis. My neurology professor said he had brain damage. He prescribed anti-epileptic drugs, even though little Harold had never had a seizure. My professor of pediatrics said he was "simply mentally retarded" and solemnly announced that he should be "put away in the developmental center at the state hospital."

It reminded me of the old story about the blind men and the elephant. The king asked two blind men to touch an elephant and tell him what it was. One touched a leg and declared it a tree; the next touched the trunk and declared it a snake. In a similar way each of my professors touched poor little Harold. Each diagnosed only what they knew, and prescribed only what they knew how to prescribe. And all I knew was that little Harold was very sick, and the nature of his disease was a complete mystery, a real challenge.

At that instant I knew exactly why Dad had made his choice. For him, the head was the most difficult part of the body to diagnose, the most mysterious, and thus the most interesting! To me, little Harold's autism was the most mysterious disease I had ever encountered in a little child, and thus the most interesting.

The answer to the second question, what kept me trying to slay the same "dragon" year after year and decade after decade is just as simple. My uncle, Dr. Joseph Weinreb, was the director of the Worcester Massachusetts Child Guidance Clinic and a professor at Clark University when I was still in medical school. He was not just my favorite uncle, but became my mentor after my father passed away from a sudden heart attack a few years after I graduated from medical school. At that time I had just started teaching at UCLA Medical School. I was on the bottom rung of the academic ladder, a lowly instructor in the division of child psychiatry.

While Uncle Joe and I lived on different coasts we would meet at least once a year at the annual meeting of the American Academy of Child Psychiatry, of which he was a founding member. Each time we met or chatted on the phone his first words weren't "Hi, how are you?" or "How's the family?" No, his first words were always the same: "Tell me what's new, what experiments are you planning on doing next year?" He kept encouraging me – his curiosity constantly refueling mine.

Also, a career in research can be addictive. As you know from reading the preceding chapters, I was fortunate to have been doing research during a time of many "dawns." I saw the dawn of computer-assisted brain recording, the dawn of neurobiochemistry, the dawn of neuropharmacology and psychoactive drug treatment, the dawn of brain imaging with MRI, PET, and CAT scans, and the dawn of molecular genetics. There was always something new and exciting to try out on our patients. And every time we discovered something new it led to a new path down our research trail that proved to be as exciting as the last. Rushing to the laboratory to see how an experiment turned out is truly a "high," an intellectual and emotional "addiction."

So I confess that I became a "research junkie." And there was Uncle Joe, spurring me along, sharing my joys and my frustrations. And the years rolled by so quickly I hardly realized that time was slipping by until, finally, it was time to retire. And that's how I kept dueling the same dragon year after year, decade after decade, with ever-increasing interest.

During my basic training in the army medical corps at Fort Sam Houston in San Antonio, Texas (which I thought was the end of the world at that time, though not now) we had a colonel who was without a shadow of a doubt the most boring, most stultifying lecturer I ever had the misery of having to listen to. And, you guessed it: his subject was "How To Give a Lecture – Army Style." During each lecture he repeated three times this "secret of successful teaching," which was "If you want to get it into their thick skulls, (1) tell 'em what you're going to tell 'em, (2) tell 'em, and then (3) tell 'em what you told 'em."

So, I guess he wasn't such a bad teacher after all. For here I am, many years later, following his advice. In Table 2 you will find a repeat of the chart of the medical model (Figure 1, chapter 1). This time I have filled in the map with more landmarks. Please look it over carefully. If it all makes sense, then I have accomplished my mission of helping you understand the nature of autism. If not, please review the relevant part of the text and I hope that will unconfuse you.

Table 2 A detailed medical model of autism and Asperger's disorder

Clinical symptoms	Brain pathology	Cause(s)	Supportive treatments
Type of onset: early vs late – same outcome	Delayed and uneven brain development	Three types: 1) unknown (80%) 2) secondary (10%) 3) familial (10%)	1) behavior therapy 2) special education 3) occupational therapy
Worldwide, no ethnic or social class differences, prevalence around 40 per 10,000	Autopsy studies: decreased purkinje cells in the cerebellum	No environment "triggers" found so far	4) medications 5) social skills training 6) coaching psychotherapy
Male female ratio 5:1	Signal processing (chemical messenger) dysfunction – serotonin, melatonin, dopamine	"Genetic loading in familial type": my "best guess" is that abnormal micro-RNA causes	7) vocational therapy 8) supported group living, estate planning
Separation of three developmental pathways: 1) sensory-motor 2) language 3) relatedness	Abnormal vestibular, and eye reflexes, sleep cycling, responses to clicks while sleeping	delays, spurts, and plateaus of brain development	9) speech and language therapy 10) marital counseling 11) sports and hobbies
Spurts and plateaus of development until age 20+	Perceptual inconstancy (over- and underreactions to sensations)	Factors that cause abnormal micro-RNA as yet unknown Radiation? Cosmic rays?	12) assistance from siblings
Four clinical types: 1) severe autism 2) mild/high-functioning autism 3) Asperger's disorder 4) subclinical type, never diagnosed	Total brain size larger during infancy		

Suggestions for Gathering Further Information

The internet is rapidly becoming the major way in which new medical and scientific information is spread. Regular scientific articles and books are frequently out of date before they are printed. With this in mind, and with my eye on the future, I am not recommending more books or articles to keep you up to date. Rather I suggest that you regularly survey several internet sites that can keep you current on autism, Asperger's disorder, and related fields. For starters, you should regularly contact the Autism Society of America (www.autism-society.org) and the National Institutes of Health website called PubMed Central (www.pubmedcentral.nih.gov). Each has search engines that will take you directly to your area of interest. The Autism Resources Organization (www.autism-resources.com) provides information and links for autism and Asperger's disorder. The National Institute of Mental Health has information on autism spectrum disorders at www.nimh.nih.gov/healthinformation/autismmenu.cfm. Next I suggest that you set up a regular search for topics you want to keep up-to-date on with major newspapers such as the *New York Times* and the *Los Angeles Times.* For instance, you could request that each time an article with the word autism in the title appears they send it to your computer. If you are not in the United States take a look at the Autism Europe site (www.autism-europe.org) or the site for the National Autistic Society of England (www.nas.org.uk). Alternatively, search on "autism society" and the country you are in, to find sites in native languages.

Finally, there are several websites devoted exclusively to autism and Asperger's disorder. They are found by typing these words in to your search engine. Because they are frequently changed I am not listing any ones at this point in time.

The internet is your library, and learning how to use it as soon as possible is the best way to keep up with the explosion of medical and scientific knowledge that is fortunately going on as I write. Let us hope that autism and Asperger's disorder will wind up in the dumpster of "cured" diseases where they can rot into historical obscurity along with polio and smallpox.

Index

Pages numbers in **bold** refer to figures, page numbers in *italics* refer to information contained in tables.